# weeknight
# vegetarian

Recipes and text  **Ivy Manning**
Photographs  **Kimberley Hasselbrink**

weldon**owen**

# Vegetarian Every Night

Whether you are adopting a Meatless Monday approach to dinner, or you're a longtime vegetarian, consistently putting a delicious, plant-based supper on the table on weeknights can be a daunting task. I find that many "quick" cookbooks revolve around meat as the center of the plate; you can flip to the vegetable section of these books and find fine recipes for side dishes or salads, but nothing that you would consider a satisfying meal.

This book is different. In the following pages, I offer 80 quick, complete dinner recipes that will help you answer the vegetarian "what's for dinner?" question, plus dozens of tips and ideas for more off-the-cuff meals. You won't find dated vegetarian recipes for "nut loaf" or recipes full of highly processed faux steak cutlets here. Instead, I focus on fresh, homemade food that just happens to be meat-free.

Since vegetarian cuisine is, by its nature, based on vegetables, I group the recipes in this book by the seasons and focus on cooking vegetables when they are at their peak. Cooking this way is inherently quick, because you don't need to do much to the ingredients to make them shine—think comforting sautéed leeks and morel mushrooms layered in a creamy quick lasagna (page 62) in spring; juicy heirloom tomatoes on grilled pizza (page 71) in summer; sweet, nutty roasted brussels sprouts on cheesy polenta (page 109) in fall; and savory quinoa and black bean cakes with juicy mango salsa (page 176) in winter.

In addition to using seasonal produce to anchor meals, I show you tasty ways to utilize plant-based proteins like canned beans, quick-cooking lentils, cheese, eggs, tofu, tempeh, and seitan, so your vegetarian dinners are as nutritious and filling as they are tasty. I also include a "vegetarian toolbox" on page 12 to explain key ingredients for vegetarian cooking, all of which will provide you with a palette of incredible flavors so that you'll never miss the meat.

I love classic American fare; so I've developed a host of recipes based on familiar comfort foods like Macaroni and Cheese with Peas and Crisp Bread Crumbs (page 34) and Mushroom Skillet Pot Pie (page 119). I've also included a generous number of recipes inspired by my travels, where I have discovered that some of the most interesting food in the world comes from cultures that either eschew meat or use meat only as a luxury ingredient. Sprinkled throughout this book you'll find recipes inspired by these cultures. Dishes like Black Bean—Avocado Sopes (page 72), Savory Japanese Vegetable Pancakes (page 142), and South Indian—Style Lentil and Vegetable Stew (page 173). All of these tasty and creative dishes will help you breathe new life into your everyday dinner repertoire. As a bonus, they are all developed with the busy cook in mind, which means you can get a delicious homemade vegetarian dinner on the table in 45 minutes or less.

Vegetarian cooking can be a smart, healthy way to eat, but this is not designed to be a diet book; rather, it is about putting quick, delicious recipes on the table that are meat-free and full of nutrients. When there's no meat on the plate, there is lots more room for vegetables, fruits, and fiber-rich grains, and those are things nearly everyone needs more of.

With this book, I hope you will find just how easy it is to put a meat-free dinner on the table, even on the busiest nights. Let this book inspire you to eat less meat, consume a wider variety of vegetables, and enjoy cooking any night of the week.

*Ivy Manning*

# What Does it Mean to Eat Vegetarian?

There are millions of people all over the world who consider themselves vegetarians, meaning they consume a diet wholly made up of vegetables, fruits, grains, nuts, and seeds. Sometimes the term "ovo-lacto vegetarian" is used to indicate the inclusion of eggs and dairy in their diets.

In addition, there are large segments of the global population who identify as vegan, which means they eat no animal products of any kind, including milk, eggs, cheese, and even honey. As awareness of the health benefits and ethics of meat consumption have increased, the notion of vegetarianism has become more flexible and more people are dipping their toes in the vegetarian waters. More and more, people are claiming that they are "vegetarian-inclined" or "flexitarian." This less-strict approach means these people choose to eat a plant-based diet most of the time. Within this casual group there are those who define themselves as "pescatarians," folks who include fish in their diet, as well as those who don't eat red meat but do eat poultry, and the witty group who label themselves "bacon-atarians." There is room for everyone at the table. This book is perfect for ovo-lacto vegetarians, but can be easily customized to include all types of people who enjoy eating a mostly plant-based diet.

## The approach of this book

While I don't personally identify as a vegetarian, I cook vegetarian meals at home because my husband (whom I affectionately call Mr. Tofu) does. When planning a meal like the ones in this book, I start with whatever vegetables are in season as the focus and add ingredients from there, perhaps starch in the form of pasta, rice, or whole grains, a bit of protein in the form of tofu, beans, or cheese or Greek yogurt, and add flavor hits like fresh herbs, hearty mushrooms, and umami-rich condiments like miso to make our meals complete. If you are already vegetarian, the recipes inside these pages will breathe new life into your daily dinner routine. If you're a vegan, you'll find a wide range of vegan recipes marked with a "v," and I give tips where applicable to make a dish vegan with a few quick substitutions or omissions.

## About Protein

The USDA recommends adults consume around 46—56 grams of protein a day depending on their activity level. That is about two 3-ounce (90-g) servings of meat or fish. As a point of reference, the average supermarket boneless chicken breast is 5—6 ounces (155—185 g) and most steaks served in restaurants are at least 8 ounces (250 g)! You can get nearly the same amount of protein without eating meat by consuming two (½-cup) servings of tofu or two 6-ounce (185-g) portions of Greek yogurt. And that doesn't include the smaller amounts of protein in vegetables, nuts, seeds, and grains.

The bottom line? As long as you are eating a varied diet of vegetables, fruits, grains, dairy, legumes, and nuts every day, it's unlikely you'll ever be protein deficient. In fact, today's medical community is generally more concerned with the chronic diseases that are related to overconsumption of protein like heart disease, kidney stones, and some types of cancer than they are worried about folks perishing from a lack of protein in their diet.

That being said, the one nutrient vegetarians—and especially vegans—need be aware of is vitamin B12. It is an essential nutrient that helps keep nerve and blood cells healthy and is key in DNA production. B12 is available in animal foods like meat, fish, poultry, eggs, and milk. Vegans can get B12 from supplements, nutritional yeast, some fortified cereals, and soy or nut milks, so as long as they're aware of the issue and eat a varied diet of fresh foods.

# The Vegetarian Toolbox

Following are a number of ingredients that have helped up my vegetarian cooking game. Some contribute protein to keep me full longer, others serve as vibrant add-ins to make my palate sing, and still others give meatless meals pleasing textures so I don't feel as if something is missing. Have these on hand and you've got a year of vegetarian dishes at your fingertips.

## Protein Stars

**Tofu**  Made from soybeans that are cooked and ground to produce soymilk, tofu is a versatile protein source for vegetarian meals. A coagulant is added to the soymilk to form curds that are then pressed to varying degrees of firmness from soft, custard-like silken tofu to spongy extra-firm tofu. In this book, I primarily call for extra-firm or firm tofu because they hold their shape when stir-fried and absorb other flavors really well.

**Baked and Fried Tofu**  Baked tofu is firm tofu that has been marinated and baked so it has a firm, chewy texture and full flavor. It's a nice go-to for quick meals, but it is generally higher in sodium than plain tofu, so I use it only occasionally. Fried tofu is a common ingredient in Asian cuisine, where it adds chewiness and richness to soups and saucy dishes. If you like, soak fried tofu briefly to remove some of the excess oil before cooking with it.

**Tempeh**  Tofu's rustic cousin, tempeh, is whole cooked soybean cakes that are inoculated with a mold (similar to the ones used in cheesemaking) and pressed into firm but slightly crumbly cakes. It's best when pan-fried and comes in plain and marinated types.

**Seitan**  Pronounced SAY-tan, this chewy vegetarian product is made from high-protein wheat flour that has had all the starch rinsed away. Seitan has a pleasantly dense, chewy texture that is a great alternative to chicken, beef, or pork in stir-fries and is often a primary ingredient in vegetarian sausages and deli slices. Since it's basically wheat gluten, seitan is not suitable for those with celiac disease or gluten intolerance or sensitivity.

**Eggs**  Although eggs got a bad rap in the past, they are an excellent source of protein and nutrients and are a perfect choice for a quick dinner. One large chicken egg provides 6 grams of protein. For the best flavor, choose locally laid eggs that are labeled "organic" and "cage-free" or "free range." I believe that eggs laid by happy and healthy hens that have free access to the outdoors taste better than those from battery-raised birds. If you can find duck eggs, give them a try; they are a rich treat.

**Greek Yogurt**  A popular choice, Greek yogurt is made thick and creamy by draining off some of the whey from traditional yogurt. Greek yogurt packs up to 3 times the protein of regular yogurt. But since there's currently no regulation on the term "Greek yogurt," some brands add starches and gums to thicken their yogurt instead of the more costly draining process used to make true Greek yogurt. Real Greek yogurt contains only milk and active live cultures and no added ingredients, so read the label. Choose low-fat versions if you're watching calories and saturated fat.

**Haloumi**  Haloumi is a firm, tangy cheese made from a combination of goat and sheep's milk. It has a high melting point, so you can sear

or grill it to gain a golden-brown crust without the cheese melting.

**Paneer**  Similar in texture to haloumi, this is a firm, white cheese made from cow's milk that is often used in Indian cuisine. Both haloumi and paneer are a good alternative to tofu if your vegetarian diet includes dairy products.

**Lentils**  Lentils are ideal for quick meals because they don't require soaking and they are tender after simmering for as little as 20 minutes. Orange and yellow lentils will melt into a silky purée when simmered. Black beluga and army-green Le Puy lentils will hold their shape once cooked, so they are ideal in pilafs, as a side dish, and in salads. Rinse all lentils well before cooking them.

**Beans**  Though soaking and simmering a pot of beans is one of the most gratifying of kitchen practices, it's not generally doable on a busy weeknight. In this book, I use canned beans for expediency's sake. Always check the label and choose canned beans that are low in sodium and be sure to drain them and rinse them well to remove excess sodium and indigestible sugars.

**Nuts**  Nuts are a powerhouse of protein, omega-3 and -6 fatty acids, fiber, and flavor. Nuts also contain a fair amount of calories, so, if you are counting calories, keep that in mind when adding nuts to dishes. Store nuts in airtight containers or bags in the freezer, or the fats in the nuts will go rancid within a short time. Toast raw nuts in a 325°F (165°C) oven, stirring frequently until aromatic, and use within one week for best flavor.

## Flavor Hits

**Vegetable Broth**  Omnivores use chicken broth in recipes to give a mild, savory flavor to soups, sauces, and grain dishes without overwhelming other ingredients. It would make sense that vegetarians could do the same with packaged vegetable broth, but I find that many of them are thicker and stronger than chicken broth and can't always be used to the same effect. It's wise to taste different brands of vegetable broth before you settle on one to keep on hand in the pantry. For quick weeknight meals, I like Imagine brand's mild, golden-hued No-Chicken Broth, which is available at many grocery stores. I also keep a bottle of Knorr's Professional Liquid Concentrated Vegetable Base in the pantry for when I need just a bit of vegetable broth quickly; look for it at restaurant-supply stores and online.

Another option is to make your own vegetable broth and store it in the freezer. For 2 quarts (2 l) of mild broth, roughly chop 1 leek, 2 large onions, 4 large carrots, and 4 celery stalks. Sauté the vegetables along with 1 bay leaf, 10 whole black peppercorns, and 1 garlic clove in 1 tablespoon canola oil until tender. Add 12 cups (96 fl oz/2.5 l) cold water and 3 dried shiitake mushrooms. Simmer for 45 minutes and strain. Season with salt or soy sauce to taste and store in an airtight container for up to 1 week in the refrigerator, or up to 3 months in the freezer.

**Fresh Herbs**  Dried herbs are handy for long-simmered soups and stews, but when you're creating quick-cooking meals, you don't have as much time to coax out their savory flavor. For this reason, in most of the recipes in this book, I call for fresh herbs. It takes minimal space to grow a little pot of thyme, rosemary, and basil and the reward is instant, fresh flavor. If you are purchasing fresh herbs, wrap them loosely in paper towels to wick away moisture and store them in the vegetable keeper in plastic bags. Their storage life will vary from a week for tender herbs like basil and tarragon to a few weeks for heartier herbs like rosemary and thyme.

**Parmesan Cheese**  Made from the milk of grass-fed cows in Northwestern Italy, authentic Parmigiano-Reggiano cheese delivers a huge amount of nutty, savory flavor in small quantities. When I call for Parmesan in this book, I'm referring to the genuine article. Be sure to keep the hard rind after using the cheese; add it to soups and sauces for extra umami.

**Fresh Mushrooms**  Mushrooms are a key ingredient in vegetarian cooking because they deliver both big, some may even say "beefy," flavor and a substantial texture that makes meals satisfying. Not all mushrooms are created equal, however. I avoid white button mushrooms because I believe they offer little in the way of flavor or texture. Instead, I opt for deeply flavored shiitake, cremini, Portobello, and wild mushrooms when available.

To clean mushrooms, avoid soaking them in water or they will become soggy. Instead, use a soft bristled toothbrush to flick away any dirt. If you must wash mushrooms, dunk them in a bowl of cold water, drain them quickly, and then gently spin them dry in a salad spinner.

**Dried Shiitake Mushrooms** I keep a stash of dried shiitake mushrooms in the pantry because they keep indefinitely and they give big, earthy flavor and a nice chewiness to stir-fries, soups, and rice dishes. To reconstitute dried mushrooms, place them in a small heatproof bowl, cover with very hot water, and soak them until they become pliable, 20—30 minutes. Discard the woody stems before using. Keep the mushroom soaking water (avoid the grit that collects on the bottom of the bowl) and add it to sauces and soups to boost their flavor.

**Konbu** A type of dried sea kelp, konbu is a popular ingredient in Japanese cooking. When it is cooked in water, the long, flat sheets release glutamates that we perceive as the savory taste sensation called "umami." Konbu is the primary component in dashi broth, the ubiquitous clear stock used in miso soup. It can also be added to dry beans to make them more digestible. Konbu is available at Asian groceries and health food stores in cellophane packages in folded 24-inch (60-cm) lengths. Don't be tempted to rinse off the white powder on the konbu; this is the glutamate salt that gives you the umami flavor you're after.

**Soy Sauce** Made from fermented soybeans, wheat, water, and salt, soy sauce is a flavor-boosting staple. I prefer good-quality aged Japanese soy sauce because it is milder and less harsh than big name brands that use chemical processes to derive soy sauce quickly and inexpensively. Try a brand like Ohsawa nama shoyu (raw, unpasteurized, aged soy sauce) and you'll be amazed at the depth of flavor and complexity compared to the stuff you get in take-out packets! Not just good for Asian food, soy sauce adds a rich, round flavor to everything from vinaigrettes to soup.

**Tamari** Similar to soy sauce, tamari is generally made without the addition of wheat, so it's ideal for those who are enjoying a gluten-free lifestyle. Tamari tends to be stronger in flavor than soy sauce. I like to use it as part of a dipping sauce.

**Miso** A thick paste made from fermented soybeans and either barley or rice, miso is packed with savory taste. There are hundreds of types of miso in Japan and the flavors vary depending on the ingredients used and age. The most common miso types in the United States are mild, sweet-salty shiro miso (white miso); coarse, red sendai miso, which is used in marinades, hearty stews, and spaghetti sauce; and dark brown, smoky hatcho miso, which is great slathered on tofu or used in strong-flavored root vegetable dishes. Stir miso into anything that needs a little umami boost, from vinaigrettes to soups to sauces. Miso keeps indefinitely in the refrigerator.

**Nutritional Yeast** Similar to brewer's yeast, nutritional yeast comes as a golden powder or fine flakes. The yeast is combined with molasses or cane sugar for flavor. The yeast is deactivated, so it won't leaven anything when introduced to moisture, but it will add a "cheesy" flavor to everything from fried tofu to popcorn. Nutritional yeast is an excellent source of vitamin B12 for vegans.

# Cooking Quick Vegetarian Meals

There is a popular misconception that vegetarian meals take longer to prepare than meat-centric ones. While there are certainly plenty of vegetarian recipes that require a day of puttering in the kitchen and long simmering, there are plenty of other meat-free recipes that can be made within 30—40 minutes. In fact, some of the recipes in this book require just 20 minutes from start to finish. Here are a few tips to get you started making quick vegetarian meals.

**Make a plan and stick to it.** Call me an overplanner, but every Sunday evening, I look at my schedule for the week and then pick out recipes I can realistically make in the 30—60 minutes I have to cook dinner. I assign one recipe for each dinner of the week and plan on using leftovers for lunches. Next, I write a shopping list with only the things I need for those recipes and shop accordingly. When five o'clock rolls around, and I'm tired and hungry, I look at my plan and know what's for dinner without giving it much thought. Try it. It works.

**Know what you have.** If you're anything like me, you might have a bit of a backstock lurking in your pantry, refrigerator, and freezer. I keep a list of what is in each place and use this as inspiration for meals when planning my week. For example, the collard greens in the vegetable keeper might meet the can of beans and rice in the pantry for a quick Southern-inspired hoppin' john (see page 166 for my easy recipe), or the red lentils I've had for awhile will go into soup with the half-head of cauliflower I need to use up.

**Make that a double.** If you make a soup, stew, sauce, or casserole that is a big hit with the family, double the recipe next time and freeze half of it. Invest in good-quality freezer-safe containers and label them clearly with the contents and the date. The borscht you loved today will be a godsend when you find a batch stored in the freezer a month later. Some of the recipes in this book that freeze well include Veggie Hot Dogs (page 79), Red Hominy Stew (page 137), Bean and Corn Enchiladas (page 127), and Broccoli and Cheddar Soup (page 179).

**Get to know your chef's knife.** Cooking a fresh, plant-based diet means you will need to spend a little more time chopping. If you're not as comfortable with your knife skills as you'd like to be, invest a few hours in a hands-on knife skills class to learn how to efficiently sharpen your knife and chop things. You'll reap the benefits every day, right around dinnertime.

**Cheat.** When time is tight, buy precut vegetables and fruit. Many grocery stores carry bags of prewashed and chopped kale, peeled and chopped winter squash, and sliced mushrooms; these and similar prepped ingredients can be incorporated into recipes on your busiest nights. You can even raid the salad bar at a health food store or upscale grocery for prepped vegetables. They cost a little more than what's uncut in the produce department, but they're super convenient in a pinch.

**Prep ahead.** If you use a lot of finely minced garlic and ginger, mince them using a mini food processor and keep them in small jars in the refrigerator. Tightly covered, minced garlic and ginger will keep for up to 10 days so you can grab what you need for a recipe.

# Cooking with the Seasons

Relying on fresh produce for your meals means you need to do little to them to help the ingredients shine. Start with what's fresh and in season at the market, and you are halfway to creating quick and easy meals any night of the week.

Another good reason to seek out seasonally available fresh fruits and vegetables is that the produce tends to taste better when it grows and thrives in its natural climate conditions. For example, while it's possible to find quality tomatoes grown in a hothouse, they're just not the same as meaty, juicy tomatoes sourced from a farmers' market in the middle of August. Buying directly from the farmers at my local market helps me feel better about supporting my local economy, which, in turn, helps me enjoy the food I prepare all the more.

In addition to what's in season, I like to keep the weather in mind when planning my meals. On a hot day I might opt for a quick, hearty sandwich or a meal that can be quickly grilled outdoors; on a cool day, I may crave a hot soup or stew to combat the cold temperatures. Use the chart at right to help inspire your own cooking throughout the year.

## Seasonal Produce

The list below provides guidance on the peak seasons for fruits, vegetables, and herbs. Local climates can vary, so the offerings may be different in your area.

### Spring

- Artichokes
- Asparagus
- Beets
- Bok choy
- Carrots
- English peas
- Fava beans
- Leeks
- Lettuces
- Meyer lemons
- New potatoes
- Pea shoots
- Sugar snap and snow peas
- Spinach
- Swiss chard
- Wild mushrooms

### Summer

- Bell peppers
- Chiles
- Corn
- Cucumbers
- Eggplants
- Green beans
- Greens: arugula and spinach
- Portobello mushrooms
- Summer squashes
- Tomatillos
- Tomatoes

### Fall

- Apples
- Broccoli
- Brussels sprouts
- Cabbage
- Cauliflower
- Chinese broccoli
- Corn
- Hearty greens: kale, chard, and mustard
- Pears
- Potatoes
- Radicchio
- Sweet potatoes
- Wild mushrooms
- Winter squashes

### Winter

- Beets
- Broccoli
- Cauliflower
- Cabbage
- Celery root
- Fennel
- Garnet yams
- Hearty greens: kale, chard, and collards
- Potatoes
- Sweet potatoes
- Watercress
- Winter squashes

# Building a Vegetarian Pantry

Having a well-stocked pantry is a boon to the busy cook, as it helps you to quickly put together meals throughout the week. Depending on what type of foods you include in your diet, stocking the pantry requires a little extra thought when you are living a vegetarian lifestyle. For example, if you love Thai and Vietnamese food, but are a practicing vegan, fish sauce is not an option for you. Instead, stock your pantry with mushroom soy sauce for a similar hit of flavor. Vegans should read the labels of Thai curry paste and Worcestershire sauce as well, to ensure they contain no fish or shellfish products.

If your cupboard is well stocked with such things as dried pastas and grains; canned beans and tomatoes; a good supply of condiments, flavoring pastes, and sauces; sea vegetables; and prepared vegetable broth, you should only need to shop a couple times a week for perishable ingredients. That being said, I don't recommend stocking up on large quantities of spices, so those are not included in the list at right. I prefer to buy spices in small quantities that I can use up relatively quickly so that they are always fresh.

The checklist at right features the pantry items that I used to build the recipes in this book. Use it as a personal checklist, or as a template for customizing your own vegetarian pantry.

## Vegetarian Pantry Checklist

Below is a list of basic kitchen staples that are used in many of the recipes in this book. Keep a supply of the following items on hand and you'll be able to make tempting vegetarian meals anytime.

### Staples

- ☐ Bulgur
- ☐ Canned beans: black, cannellini, chickpeas, kidney
- ☐ Coconut milk
- ☐ Cooking oils: canola, olive
- ☐ Dried mushrooms
- ☐ Flour: all-purpose, whole wheat, cornmeal, masa harina
- ☐ Hominy
- ☐ Lentils
- ☐ Olives
- ☐ Panko bread crumbs
- ☐ Pasta: fregola, penne, linguine, no-boil lasagna sheets, rotini, shells, spaghetti
- ☐ Peanut butter
- ☐ Polenta
- ☐ Quinoa
- ☐ Rice: Arborio, jasmine, long-grain, short grain, quick-cooking wild
- ☐ Rice noodles: cellophane, wide noodles
- ☐ Roasted red peppers
- ☐ Sea vegetables: konbu, nori, wakame
- ☐ Tomatillos
- ☐ Tomato products: fire-roasted diced, sauce, paste, marinara sauce, San Marzano
- ☐ White miso
- ☐ Wine: Chinese rice, dry white, mirin, Marsala, sherry

### Condiments & Sauces

- ☐ Black bean garlic sauce
- ☐ Chile sauce: gochujang, Sriracha, sweet red
- ☐ Chipotle chiles in adobo
- ☐ Flavoring oils: Asian chile, toasted sesame, truffle
- ☐ Hot-pepper sauce
- ☐ Indian-style curry paste
- ☐ Ketchup
- ☐ Kimchi
- ☐ Massaman curry paste
- ☐ Mayonnaise
- ☐ Mustard: Dijon and grainy
- ☐ Nutritional yeast
- ☐ Soy sauce: regular, mushroom, tamari
- ☐ Thai-style curry paste: red and green
- ☐ Vegetable broth
- ☐ Vegetarian worcestershire
- ☐ Vinegars: balsamic, Chinese black, cider, red wine, rice, sherry

# Spring

# Spring

Spring is a breath of fresh air on a plate. After a winter of heavy roasted roots and stews, it's such a relief to shift into lightness—slender asparagus spears, verdant snow peas, and leafy greens that need only a quick dunk in boiling water or a few seconds in a hot pan. Wild mushrooms find their way into herby crepes and pasta dishes, and there are quick-cooking peas for creamy risotto, leeks for gratins, and buttery fava beans for nearly everything.

## Smart Strategies for Spring Meals

- The best way to highlight tender spring vegetables is to blanch them—dunk them in a pot of boiling water until tender-crisp (usually 1—2 minutes) and then plunge them into a bowl of ice water to stop the cooking. Drain and dress with vinaigrette.

- Tender herbs—like anise-like tarragon, aromatic lemon thyme, tangy dill, and oniony chives—are great complements to spring vegetables. Consider planting small pots of these essential herbs and keeping them on your kitchen windowsill.

- Handle spring's leafy greens with a light hand and they'll stay fresh longer. To wash bunches of beet greens, lettuces, and chard, untie them, plunge them in a clean sink of cool water, swish to remove any soil or pests, and then spin them dry in a salad spinner. Store washed greens in the vegetable crisper in plastic bags with a few paper towels inside to wick away moisture; use within 1 week.

- Sprightly citrus zest brings out the lush, grassy flavors of spring meals. To get every last drop of flavor from citrus zest, use a sharp rasp grater and hold the fruit over the food to capture the essential oils that are released as you grate.

## Super-Simple Spring Side Dishes

- Coat asparagus with olive oil and grill until lightly charred. Toss with lemon juice, salt, and pepper. Shave Parmigiano-Reggiano cheese over the top.

- Toss baby spinach with sliced strawberries and almonds and a simple dressing of plain Greek yogurt, honey, and poppy seeds.

- Cook 1½ cups (10½ oz/330 g) long-grain rice as directed on the package. Off the heat stir in ¼ cup (⅓ oz/10 g) chopped fresh Italian parsley, ¼ cup (1 oz/30 g) chopped pistachios, and 2 tablespoons each of chopped fresh tarragon, dill, and mint.

- Cut pea shoots into 2-inch (5-cm) lengths and stir-fry them briefly with sliced shiitake mushrooms, a squeeze of lime juice, and a drizzle of soy sauce.

- Trim away the greens from 2 bunches of radishes. Halve the radishes, toss with olive oil, and roast in a 450°F (230°C) oven until tender, about 15 minutes. Toss with cultured butter and fresh sea salt.

- Toss mixed baby lettuces from the farmers' market with fresh berries, toasted nuts, and crumbled blue cheese. Toss with a tarragon vinaigrette.

This eggs-for-dinner recipe requires very few ingredients, so buy the best farm-fresh eggs and baby spinach you can find. Serve with warm sourdough bread and a crisp, dry white wine like a Spanish Albariño.

# Creamy Eggs Florentine with Crispy Sourdough Crumbs

**Small sourdough roll or slice of rustic sourdough bread,** 1, torn into small pieces

**Extra-virgin olive oil,** 2 tablespoons

**Fresh thyme,** 2 teaspoons chopped

**Sea salt and freshly ground pepper**

**Shallots,** ¼ cup (1¼ oz/45 g) thinly sliced

**Garlic,** 2 teaspoons minced

**Baby spinach,** ½ lb (250 g)

**Large eggs,** 8

**Heavy cream,** 1 cup (8 fl oz/250 ml)

**Fresh tarragon,** 2 teaspoons chopped

**Freshly grated nutmeg**

**MAKES 4 SERVINGS**

1   Preheat the oven to 375°F (190°C). Spray two 4-cup (32–fl oz/1-l capacity) gratin dishes with cooking spray and place them on a rimmed baking sheet.

2   Pulse the bread in a food processor or chop with a chef's knife until coarse crumbs form. In a sauté pan, warm 1 tablespoon of the oil over medium heat. Add the bread crumbs, thyme, and a sprinkle each of salt and pepper, and cook, stirring constantly, until the bread crumbs are browned and crisp, about 5 minutes. Scrape the bread crumbs onto a plate.

3   Wipe out the sauté pan and return it to medium-high heat. Add the remaining 1 tablespoon oil. Add the shallots and garlic and sauté until they begin to brown, 45 seconds. Add the spinach by the handful and toss with tongs until it is wilted, 2 minutes. Season with a pinch of salt. Place the spinach in the 2 gratin dishes. Crack 4 eggs into each dish, spacing them evenly. Pour the cream around the eggs and sprinkle with the tarragon, a small pinch of nutmeg, and a little salt and pepper. Bake, rotating the baking dishes once, until the egg whites are set and the yolks are slightly runny, about 12 to 15 minutes.

4   Remove the dishes from the oven. Sprinkle the toasted bread crumbs over the dishes, dividing evenly, and serve right away.

You're looking for irregular bits of freshly ground bread crumbs to add texture here, so don't opt for purchased dry bread crumbs.

This recipe is very adaptable. You can substitute sautéed mushrooms, zucchini, or tomatoes for the spinach; in fact, just about any tender vegetable will taste great in this recipe.

In this vegetarian version of the Vietnamese baguette sandwich, I use slices of marinated tofu instead of the traditional pâté. Add crunchy vegetables and a quick, spicy mayonnaise and you'll never miss the meat.

# Lemongrass Tofu Bánh Mì

**Fresh lemongrass,** 1 tablespoon finely chopped (white bulb part only)

**Garlic,** 1 tablespoon finely chopped

**Sriracha sauce,** 2 teaspoons

**Lime juice,** 2 teaspoons

**Sugar,** 2 teaspoons

**Sea salt and freshly ground pepper**

**Canola oil,** ¼ cup (2 fl oz/60 ml) plus 2 tablespoons

**Extra-firm tofu,** 1 lb (500 g), patted dry and cut into slabs ¼ inch (6 mm) thick

**Mayonnaise,** ½ cup (4 fl oz/125 ml)

**Daikon,** ¾ cup (4 oz/125 g) grated

**Carrot,** ¾ cup (4 oz/125 g) grated

**Rice vinegar,** 1 tablespoon

**Vietnamese-style soft baguette rolls or hoagie buns,** 4

**Fresh cilantro leaves,** 1 cup (1 oz/30 g)

**Large jalapeño chile,** 1, thinly sliced

**MAKES 4 SERVINGS**

To make the thin vegetable cuts for this recipe, consider investing in a julienne peeler, a handy rake-like device that makes perfect julienne strips out of firm vegetables like daikon and carrot. Look for them at kitchenware stores and online.

✕

Because lemongrass is a tough stem to chop, I like to buy packaged minced lemongrass, sold at Asian markets and in the produce section of some specialty food stores.

1 In a mini food processor or using a mortar and pestle, pulse or pound the lemongrass, garlic, Sriracha, lime juice, and 1 teaspoon of the sugar with ½ teaspoon each salt and pepper until a paste forms. Add 2 tablespoons of the oil and blend well. Coat the tofu pieces using 3 tablespoons of the lemongrass paste; set aside. Mix together the remaining paste and the mayonnaise and set aside.

2 In a small bowl, combine the daikon, carrot, remaining 1 teaspoon sugar, and the rice vinegar with ½ teaspoon salt; set aside. In a large nonstick frying pan, warm the remaining ¼ cup (2 fl oz/60 ml) oil over medium-high heat. Add the tofu and fry until golden-brown and crisp, 2 minutes per side. Transfer to a paper towel–lined plate.

3 Cut open the rolls horizontally, leaving one long side of the bun partially attached. Spread the mayonnaise evenly on the inside of the rolls. Place the tofu on the buns and top with the daikon-carrot salad, cilantro, and jalapeños. Serve right away.

(V) This salad of crisp vegetables, crunchy tempeh, and curry-cashew dip is the perfect meal when you've overindulged. Feel free to play with the vegetables and fruits according to the season and your whim.

# Indonesian-Style Vegetable Salad with Tempeh

**Jasmine rice,** 1 cup (7 oz/220 g)

**Turmeric,** ½ teaspoon

**Sea salt**

**Roasted salted cashews,** ½ cup (2½ oz/75 g)

**Lime juice,** ¼ cup (2 fl oz/60 ml)

**Soy sauce,** 1 tablespoon

**Thai red curry paste,** 1 tablespoon

**Brown sugar,** 1 tablespoon

**Broccoli florets,** 2 cups (4 oz/125 g)

**Green beans,** 1 cup (6 oz/180 g), cut into 2-inch (5 cm) lengths

**Cucumber,** 1, halved lengthwise and cut into ¼-inch (6-mm) slices

**Fresh pineapple chunks,** 1 cup (6 oz/185 g)

**Red bell pepper,** ½, seeded and thinly sliced

**Canola oil,** 1½ tablespoons

**Marinated tempeh strips** (I like Tofurky Coconut Curry flavor), ½ lb (250 g)

**MAKES 4 SERVINGS**

1 In a small saucepan, combine the rice, turmeric, ½ teaspoon salt, and 2 cups (16 fl oz/500 ml) water. Bring to a boil, reduce the heat to low, cover, and simmer until tender, 15 minutes.

2 In a food processor, combine ¼ cup (4 fl oz/125 ml) hot water with the cashews, lime juice, soy sauce, curry paste, and brown sugar, and process until smooth. Pour the mixture into a small serving bowl and set aside.

3 Bring a saucepan of water to a boil. Fill a bowl with ice water. Add the broccoli to the boiling water and cook for 2 minutes. Add the green beans and cook until the beans are tender-crisp, 2 minutes. Drain the vegetables and plunge them into the ice water to stop them from overcooking. Once cool, drain the vegetables and pat dry with paper towels. On a large platter, arrange the broccoli, green beans, cucumber, pineapple, and bell pepper.

4 In a large nonstick frying pan, warm the canola oil over medium-high heat. Add the tempeh strips and cook until golden-brown and crisp, 2 minutes per side. Drain on paper towels and arrange on the platter. Serve with the cashew sauce for dipping and rice on the side.

You can skip the chopping and blanching by visiting the salad bar at your local market: Just fill a to-go container with your favorite vegetables, bring them home, and arrange them on a platter with the tempeh and dipping sauce.

This quick version of macaroni and cheese is always a crowd pleaser thanks to the creamy, tangy sauce and crispy topping. Since it's baked in the same pan the sauce is made in, it's a quick and easy clean-up, too.

# Macaroni and Cheese with Peas and Crisp Bread Crumbs

To serve this dish in individual gratin dishes (as pictured) divide the pasta mixture among 4 (2-cup/16–fl oz/500-ml) gratin dishes. Top with the bread crumbs and bake for 15 minutes. For extra crispy bread crumbs, set the baking dishes under the broiler for 30 seconds at the end of the baking time.

✕

It's wise to keep fresh bread crumbs on hand in the freezer for casseroles like this. I make bread crumbs from heels of sliced bread, and even extra hot-dog and hamburger buns. Fresh bread crumbs keep in sealable freezer bags for up to 3 months.

**Bread roll or sliced bread,** 2¼ oz (65 g), torn into pieces

**Parmesan cheese,** ¼ cup (1 oz/30 g) grated

**Extra-virgin olive oil,** 2 tablespoons

**All-purpose flour,** 3 tablespoons

**Dry mustard,** 1½ teaspoons

**Sea salt and freshly ground black pepper**

**Reduced-fat milk,** 3 cups (24 fl oz/ 750 ml)

**Dried bay leaf,** 1

**Garlic,** 1 clove, peeled and lightly smashed

**Medium shell-shaped pasta,** ¾ lb (375 g)

**Fresh, or frozen and thawed, shelled peas,** 1 cup (6 oz/190 g)

**Sharp Cheddar cheese,** 1½ cups (6 oz/185 g) grated

**Cayenne pepper,** 2 pinches

**MAKES 4–6 SERVINGS**

1 In a food processor, pulse the bread until fine crumbs form. Add the Parmesan and oil and pulse a few times to combine; set aside.

2 Preheat the oven to 350°F (180°C). Bring a large pot of water to a boil. Meanwhile, in an ovenproof saucepan, whisk together the flour, mustard, and ¾ teaspoon salt. Gradually whisk in ¼ cup (2 fl oz/60 ml) of the milk until smooth. Whisk in the remaining milk and add the bay leaf and garlic. Bring to a simmer over medium heat, whisking constantly. Reduce the heat to medium-low and simmer, whisking frequently, until the sauce is thickened and bubbly, 5 minutes. Keep warm over low heat.

3 Add the pasta to the boiling water and cook until al dente, about 7 minutes. Add the peas during the last 4 minutes if using fresh peas, or during the last minute of cooking if using thawed frozen peas. Drain the pasta and peas.

4 Remove the garlic and bay leaf from the sauce. Add the cheese to the sauce a handful at a time, whisking until fully melted before adding more. Season with the cayenne and salt and pepper to taste. Gently stir in the pasta and peas. Sprinkle evenly with the bread crumb mixture. Slide the pan into the oven, and bake until the crumbs are golden and crisp, 15—20 minutes.

(V) This Japanese-inspired noodle dish is perfect to highlight asparagus at its peak in early spring. Wakame, a deep-green sea vegetable, adds a briny counterpoint to the slippery noodles and crisp asparagus spears.

# Soba Noodles with Asparagus, Shiitake, and Wakame

**Dried wakame or mixed sea vegetables,** 2 tablespoons

**Soy sauce,** 2 tablespoons

**Rice vinegar,** 2 tablespoons

**Sugar,** 1 tablespoon

**Toasted sesame oil,** 2 teaspoons

**Soba noodles,** ½ lb (250 g)

**Canola oil,** 2 tablespoons

**Fresh ginger,** 2 teaspoons finely grated

**Garlic,** 2 teaspoons finely chopped

**Asparagus spears,** ¾ lb (375 g), tough ends snapped off and spears cut into 2-inch (5-cm) lengths

**Shiitake mushrooms,** 1 cup (3 oz/ 90 g), stems discarded and caps sliced

**MAKES 4 SERVINGS**

1 In a bowl, combine the wakame with 1 cup (8 fl oz/250 ml) cold water. Set aside to reconstitute for 15 minutes.

2 Drain the wakame, squeeze out the excess water, and set aside. In a small bowl, whisk the soy sauce, vinegar, sugar, and sesame oil until the sugar dissolves; set aside.

3 Bring a pot of water to a boil. Add the soba noodles and cook until just tender, about 4 minutes. Drain and rinse with cool water to stop them from overcooking; set aside.

4 In a wok or large nonstick frying pan, warm the canola oil over medium-high heat. Add the ginger and garlic and stir-fry until aromatic, 20 seconds. Add the asparagus and mushrooms and stir-fry, 1 minute. Add 2 tablespoons water, cover, and cook until the asparagus is tender-crisp and bright green, about 2 minutes, depending on their thickness.

5 Uncover, remove the pan from heat, and add the noodles and soy sauce mixture, tossing to coat. Divide the noodle-vegetable mixture among shallow bowls. Top the noodles with the wakame and serve warm or chilled.

Soba noodles come in a variety of types, from 100% buckwheat to a mix of mostly white flour with some buckwheat added for color. The more buckwheat in the noodles, the more intense their flavor—and the higher their price tag. If you're crunched for time, you can substitute fresh yakisoba (available in the produce department of most grocery stores) for the soba: Just drop the precooked noodles directly into the wok to reheat them.

✕

Look for dried wakame or mixed sea vegetable packets at natural foods markets and Asian stores—they're well worth the hunt!

Earthy beet greens become meltingly tender when simmered with sliced beets in broth. I add penne, creamy goat cheese, and crunchy walnuts to make a bunch of beets a satisfying meal in about 30 minutes.

# Golden Beet, Toasted Walnut, and Goat Cheese Penne

**Golden beets,** 1 bunch, greens attached (about 1 lb/500 g)

**Olive oil,** 1 tablespoon

**Unsalted butter,** 1 tablespoon

**Coriander seeds,** 2 teaspoons lightly crushed

**Garlic,** 1 large clove, thinly sliced

**Vegetable broth,** ½ cup (4 fl oz/125 ml)

**Penne pasta,** ¾ lb (375 g)

**Goat cheese or creamy feta cheese,** ¼ lb (125 g)

**Toasted walnuts,** ½ cup (2 oz/60 g), roughly chopped

**Sea salt and freshly ground pepper**

**MAKES 4 SERVINGS**

To peel beets quickly, try holding a beet in your hand and pulling the peeler towards you, as you would pare an apple.

1 Separate the beets from their greens; discard the stems. Peel the beets and cut them into ¼-inch (6-mm) wedges. In a large bowl of cold water, wash the greens, then spin them dry in a salad spinner. Transfer the greens to a cutting board and chop them coarsely.

2 In a large sauté pan, warm the oil and butter over medium heat. Add the beets and coriander seeds and sauté, 3 minutes. Add the beet greens and garlic and cook, stirring constantly with tongs, until the garlic is aromatic and the greens begin to wilt, 1 minute. Add the broth, cover, reduce the heat to medium-low, and simmer until the beets are tender when pierced with a fork, 10 minutes.

3 Meanwhile, bring a large pot of salted water to a boil and cook the penne according to package instructions. Reserving ½ cup (4 fl oz/125 ml) of the cooking liquid, drain the pasta. Add the penne, pasta cooking liquid, cheese, and walnuts to the pan with the beets, and toss to coat the pasta evenly. Season to taste with salt and pepper. Serve right away.

In this recipe, herbed crepes are packed with sautéed mushrooms and additional herbs and topped with a simple Gruyère-laden "sauce." Serve them with a butter-lettuce and fresh-pea salad with Dijon vinaigrette.

# Mushroom, Herb, and Gruyère Crepes

Herbed Crepes, page 184

Unsalted butter, 2 tablespoons

Shallots, ¾ cup (3¾ oz/115 g) thinly sliced

Mixed wild and cultivated mushrooms, ¾ lb (375 g)

Fresh thyme, 2½ teaspoons chopped

Fresh tarragon, 2 teaspoons chopped

Sea salt and freshly ground pepper

Dry white wine or vermouth, ½ cup (4 fl oz/125 ml)

Crème fraîche or sour cream, ½ cup (4 oz/125 g)

Gruyère cheese, 1 cup (3 oz/90 g) shredded

MAKES 4 SERVINGS

Choose a mixture of mushrooms such as cremini, shiitake, oyster, morel, and chanterelle.

✖

Don't overcrowd the mushrooms in the pan or they will sweat instead of brown. You'll need a large sauté pan. When in doubt, sauté the mushrooms in two batches.

1 Follow the instructions on page 184 to make the crepe batter. Set the batter aside while you make the filling.

2 In a large sauté pan, melt the butter over medium-high heat. Add the shallots and sauté until browned, about 3 minutes. Add the mushrooms, thyme, tarragon, and a generous pinch of salt and sauté until the mushrooms begin to brown, about 4 minutes. Add the wine and simmer until evaporated, about 1 minute. Season with to taste with salt and pepper.

3 Continue to follow the directions on page 184 to cook the crepes and place them in the oven to keep warm.

4 When you are ready to assemble, remove the crepes from the oven. Arrange the oven rack in the top third of the oven and preheat the broiler. Spray a 9-by-13-inch (23-by-33-cm) baking dish with cooking spray.

5 Lay the crepes on a clean work surface and place about 2½ tablespoons of the mushroom mixture on the bottom third of each crepe. Roll up the crepes and place them seam-side down in the dish. Spread the crème fraîche evenly over the tops of the crepes and sprinkle them with the cheese. Broil until the cheese is bubbly and browned, 4 minutes. Serve right away.

(V) You can throw this easy and authentic-tasting stir-fry together in minutes. Chewy seitan takes the place of meat, and umami-rich black bean–garlic sauce makes a quick, deeply flavorful seasoning sauce.

# Seitan and Vegetable Stir-Fry with Black Bean–Garlic Sauce

**Black bean–garlic sauce,** 3 tablespoons

**Chinese rice wine or dry sherry,** 2 tablespoons

**Soy sauce,** 1 tablespoon

**Cornstarch,** 2 teaspoons

**Canola oil,** 2 tablespoons

**Seitan,** ½ lb (250 g), drained and thinly sliced

**Fresh ginger,** 1 tablespoon finely chopped

**Baby bok choy,** 2 large heads, white stems cut into 1-inch (2.5-cm) slices, greens left whole

**Small red bell pepper,** 1, seeded and sliced

**Shiitake mushrooms,** 1½ cups (4 oz/125 g), stems discarded and caps sliced

**Steamed rice,** for serving

**MAKES 4 SERVINGS**

1 In a small bowl, whisk together the black bean–garlic sauce, rice wine, soy sauce, cornstarch, and 2 tablespoons water; set aside.

2 In a wok or large frying pan, warm 1 tablespoon of the oil over high heat. When the oil is nearly smoking, add the seitan and stir-fry until it is lightly seared around the edges, 1 minute. Transfer to a bowl; set aside. Reduce the heat to medium-high and add the remaining 1 tablespoon oil. Add the ginger and stir-fry until aromatic, 10 seconds. Add the bok choy, bell pepper, and mushrooms and stir-fry until the vegetables are tender-crisp, 2 minutes.

3 Return the seitan to the wok. Stir in the black bean–garlic sauce mixture, and stir-fry until the sauce is thick and bubbly, 1 minute. Serve with the rice.

Chinese black bean–garlic sauce is an ideal condiment for vegetarian cooking because the fermented black beans add a big punch of umami flavor with just a small amount. Try the sauce thinned with vinegar and oil as a dressing for steamed vegetables or egg noodles, as a marinade or rub for tofu, or as the base of a stir-fry sauce. An opened jar of black bean-garlic sauce will last for months in the refrigerator. Lee Kum Kee is the most widely available brand.

A combination of fresh chard leaves, canned pinto beans, and roasted red peppers transforms the usual cheese-centric quesadilla into a satisfying meal packed with healthy vegetables and protein.

# Swiss Chard, Pinto Bean, and White Cheddar Quesadillas

**Extra-virgin olive oil,** 1 tablespoon plus 2 teaspoons

**Shallot,** ½ cup (2½ oz/75 g) thinly sliced

**Swiss chard leaves,** ½ bunch, tough stems discarded, leaves chopped (about 5 cups/10 oz/315 g)

**Ground cumin,** ¾ teaspoon

**Sea salt**

**Large flour tortillas** (10-inch/25-cm), 4

**White Cheddar cheese,** 1½ cups (5 oz/155 g) shredded

**Pinto beans,** 1 can (15 oz/425 g), rinsed and drained

**Jarred roasted red pepper,** ¼ cup (1½ oz/45 g) thinly sliced

**Sour cream,** ½ cup (4 oz/125 g)

**Hot-pepper sauce,** 1 tablespoon

**MAKES 4 SERVINGS**

1 Preheat the oven to 200°F (95°C). In a large sauté pan or frying pan, warm the 1 tablespoon oil over medium-high heat. Add the shallot and sauté until tender and beginning to caramelize, 3 minutes. Add the chard, cumin, and a few pinches of salt and cook, stirring with tongs, until the chard is wilted, 4 minutes. Transfer to a bowl.

2 Wipe out the sauté pan. Add 1 teaspoon of the oil to the pan and warm over medium heat. Lay a tortilla flat in the pan and sprinkle evenly with one-fourth each of the cheese, chard mixture, beans, and red pepper. Cook until the bottom of the tortilla is lightly browned and the cheese has melted, 3 minutes. Fold the tortilla in half to make a half-moon shape and, using a spatula, press down to adhere. Transfer the quesadilla to a baking sheet and keep warm in the oven. Repeat the process with the remaining ingredients to make 4 quesadillas, reducing the heat if the tortillas brown too quickly.

3 In a small serving bowl, combine the sour cream and hot sauce. Cut the quesadillas into 4 wedges each, transfer them to plates, and pass the sour cream sauce separately for dipping.

To expedite this already-quick dinner, cook all the quesadillas at once on a gas grill set to medium heat.

I bake this custardy vegetable pudding in individual gratin dishes so that they are ready in only 20 minutes (a large bread pudding can take up to an hour). Serve this with a simple watercress and orange salad.

# Savory Bread Pudding with Spring Vegetables and Herbs

If you can't find fresh morel mushrooms, substitute 1 ounce (30 g) of dried morels reconstituted in 1 cup (8 fl oz/250 ml) very hot water for 30 minutes.

✕

The gratins can be assembled up to 4 hours in advance and stored in the refrigerator until you're ready to bake them.

**Day-old artisan bread,** ½ lb (250 g), crusts cut off, bread cut into ¾-inch (2-cm) cubes

**Unsalted butter,** 1 tablespoon

**Thin asparagus,** ½ lb (250 g), tough ends snapped off and stalks cut into 1-inch (2.5-cm) pieces

**Morel mushrooms,** ¼ lb (125 g), sliced

**Fresh thyme,** 1 teaspoon chopped

**Large eggs,** 6

**Heavy cream,** ¾ cup (6 fl oz/180 ml)

**Milk,** ¾ cup (6 fl oz/180 ml)

**Fresh chives,** 2 tablespoons minced

**Fresh basil,** 1 tablespoon chopped

**Fresh tarragon,** 1½ teaspoons chopped

**Lemon zest,** 1½ teaspoons finely grated

**Ground white pepper,** ¼ teaspoon

**Freshly grated nutmeg,** ⅛ teaspoon

**Sea salt**

**Parmesan cheese,** ½ cup (4 oz/125 g) grated

**MAKES 4 SERVINGS**

1 Preheat the oven to 375°F (190°C). Spray four 2-cup (16–fl oz/500-ml) gratin dishes or shallow baking dishes with cooking spray and place them on a rimmed baking sheet. Divide the bread cubes evenly among the dishes.

2 In a large sauté pan, melt the butter over medium heat. Add the asparagus, mushrooms, and thyme, and sauté until the vegetables are just tender, 3 minutes. Spread the vegetables over the bread cubes, dividing evenly.

3 In a large bowl, whisk together the eggs, heavy cream, milk, chives, basil, tarragon, lemon zest, white pepper, nutmeg, and ¼ teaspoon salt. Pour the egg mixture into the gratin dishes, dividing evenly. Using the back of a large spoon, press the bread and vegetables down so the bread absorbs the egg mixture. Sprinkle the cheese over the top. Bake until the puddings are set in the center and a butter knife inserted into the center comes out clean, 20—25 minutes. Serve warm.

This dish combines the soothing warmth of miso soup with crispy-chewy vegetable dumplings to make a satisfying meal in minutes. Set out large Asian-style soup spoons and chopsticks to pick up the dumplings.

# Miso Soup with Vegetable Gyoza

**Dried kelp (konbu) pieces,** 2 (6-inch/15-cm) pieces

**Shiitake mushrooms,** 1 cup (3 oz/90 g), stems removed and caps thinly sliced

**Frozen shelled edamame,** ¾ cup (3¾ oz/115 g)

**Canola oil,** 2 teaspoons

**Frozen vegetarian gyoza dumplings,** 1 lb (500 g)

**White (shiro) miso,** ⅓ cup (3 oz/90 g)

**Green onions,** ¼ cup (¾ oz/20 g) thinly sliced

**Soy sauce,** 1–2 tablespoons

**MAKES 4 SERVINGS**

1 In a saucepan, place the kelp, mushrooms, and edamame. Add 8 cups (64 fl oz/2 l) cold water and bring to a simmer over medium-high heat. As soon as the water begins to bubble vigorously, remove and discard the kelp.

2 In a large nonstick sauté pan, warm the oil over medium-high heat. Add the dumplings and cook until browned and crisp on the bottom, 10 minutes.

3 Place the miso in a small bowl. Ladle 1 cup (8 fl oz/250 ml) of the kelp broth into the bowl and whisk until smooth. Return the mixture to the saucepan. Add the green onions and soy sauce to taste.

4 Divide the dumplings among 4 soup bowls. Ladle the hot soup over the dumplings and serve.

Instead of making your own konbu broth, you can use instant vegetarian dashi broth, found at markets that specialize in Japanese food. Follow the package instructions, adding water to the dashi base as directed. Be sure to taste the soup before adding any soy sauce, as many instant broths are already quite salty.

This Spanish egg-and-potato dish gets an update here with buttery fava beans and a sweet-smoky red pepper dip. Serve warm or at room temperature with a butter lettuce salad with grated Manchego cheese.

# Spanish Tortilla with Favas, Asparagus, and Romesco

Romesco sauce is a classic red-pepper-and-almond—based puréed sauce from Spain. Leftover romesco makes a delicious sandwich spread or dip for crudités.

✕

Fresh fava beans require a two-step preparation: removing the beans from their pods and then peeling the beans from their rubbery skins. To save time, buy frozen shelled and skinned fava beans, which are often available at Asian and Middle Eastern markets. Use 1¼ cups (7¼ oz/230 g) frozen shelled favas for this recipe.

**Jarred roasted red bell peppers,** 1 cup (6 oz/185 g) drained

**Marcona almonds or slivered toasted almonds,** 2 tablespoons

**Sherry vinegar or red wine vinegar,** 1½ teaspoons

**Garlic,** 1 teaspoon minced

**Sweet smoked paprika,** ¼ teaspoon

**Extra-virgin olive oil,** 2 tablespoons

**Yukon gold potatoes,** 3, cut into ⅛-inch (3-mm) slices

**Sea salt and freshly ground pepper**

**Fava bean pods,** 2½ lb (1.25 kg) (about 1¼ cups/7¼ oz/230 g shelled beans)

**Large eggs,** 8

**Green onions,** 2, thinly sliced

**MAKES 2 SERVINGS**

1 In a blender or food processor, combine the roasted peppers, nuts, vinegar, garlic, and paprika with 1 tablespoon oil and blend until smooth. Set aside.

2 In a small saucepan, cover the potatoes with cold water by 2 inches (5 cm). Add 1 teaspoon salt, bring to a simmer over medium heat, and cook until easily pierced with a fork, 4 minutes. Drain and set aside. Refill the pan with water and bring to a boil. Shell the fava beans, add them to the boiling water, and cook for 2 minutes. Drain the beans and rinse them with cold water. Peel away and discard the tough, pastel-green skin from the beans.

3 In a bowl, whisk the eggs and green onions with ½ teaspoon salt and ¼ teaspoon pepper. Stir in the fava beans. Spray a 10-inch (25-cm) nonstick frying pan with cooking spray and add the remaining 1 tablespoon oil; warm over medium-high heat. Add the egg mixture and the potatoes to the pan and flatten with a spatula to even out the top. Reduce the heat to medium-low, cover, and cook until the top is nearly set, 10 minutes.

4 Remove the pan from the heat. Carefully place a dinner plate on top of the pan. Wearing oven mitts, invert the pan so the cooked side of the tortilla is facing up. Slide the tortilla back into the pan, uncooked side down, and cook until set in the center and lightly browned on the bottom, about 2 minutes. Transfer to a plate, cut into wedges, and serve with the romesco.

Haloumi has a satisfying chewiness, so it's a great substitute for meat. The cheese can be seared in a pan just as you would chicken or other animal protein. A nutty, vegetable-packed pilaf makes this a full meal.

# Fava Bean and Spinach Pilaf with Fried Haloumi

**Fava bean pods,** 2½ lb (1.25 kg) (about 1¼ cups/7¼ oz/230 g shelled beans)

**Unsalted butter,** 1 tablespoon

**Slivered almonds,** ½ cup (2 oz/60 g)

**Olive oil,** 2 tablespoons

**Leeks,** 2, white and light green parts, halved lengthwise and thinly sliced (2 cups/6 oz/185 g)

**Garlic,** 1 teaspoon finely chopped

**Long-grain rice,** 1½ cups (10½ oz/330 g)

**Vegetable broth,** 3 cups (24 fl oz/750 ml)

**Dried dill,** 1 teaspoon

**Ground cinnamon and allspice,** ¼ teaspoon *each*

**Dried bay leaf,** 1

**Chopped baby spinach,** 4 cups (8 oz/250 g), loosely packed

**Haloumi,** ½ lb (250 g), sliced into ¼-inch (6-mm) slabs and patted dry

**Fresh flat-leaf Italian parsley,** ½ cup (¾ oz/20 g) chopped

**Lemon zest,** 2 teaspoons finely grated

**Sea salt and freshly ground pepper**

MAKES 4–6 SERVINGS

If you can't find fresh fava beans (or don't want to go to the trouble to prep them), look for frozen, shelled fava beans at natural food markets and stores that carry Middle Eastern foods, then thaw them before adding them to the rice. Alternatively, you could also substitute the same amount of frozen shelled edamame for the fava beans.

1 Prepare the favas according to the instructions on page 48. In a large saucepan with a tight-fitting lid, melt the butter over medium heat. Add the almonds and cook, stirring, until the butter and almonds are golden-brown and smell nutty, 1½ minutes; scrape into a bowl and set aside.

2 In the saucepan, warm the oil over medium heat. Add the leeks and sauté until translucent, 3 minutes. Add the garlic and sauté for 45 seconds. Stir in the rice and cook, stirring constantly, for 1 minute. Add the broth, dill, cinnamon, allspice, and bay leaf, and bring to a simmer. Reduce the heat to medium-low, cover, and simmer for 10 minutes. Gently fold the favas and spinach into the rice. Cover and cook until the rice is tender, about 8 minutes.

3 Meanwhile, in a nonstick frying pan, fry the haloumi slices over medium-high heat until lightly browned, 2 minutes per side.

4 Stir the parsley, almonds, and lemon zest into the rice. Season to taste with salt and pepper, keeping in mind that the cheese is quite salty on its own. Serve the rice with the haloumi on the side.

Who doesn't love a gooey reuben stacked high with fillings? This healthy version uses seitan instead of corned beef and simmers it with the classic pickling spices. The results are equally delicious as the original.

# Vegetarian Reubens

**Mayonnaise,** 3 tablespoons

**Dill pickles,** 2 tablespoons chopped

**Ketchup,** 2 tablespoons

**Prepared horseradish,** 1 tablespoon

**Freshly ground pepper,** ¼ teaspoon

**Low-sodium vegetable broth,** 1¼ cups (10 fl oz/310 ml)

**Pickling spices,** 4 teaspoons

**Seitan,** ½ lb (250 g), cut into 4 large chunks

**Rye bread,** 8 slices

**Swiss cheese,** 8 slices

**Sauerkraut,** 1 cup (8 oz/250 g), rinsed and drained

**Unsalted butter,** 1 tablespoon

**MAKES 4 SERVINGS**

1 To make the dressing, in a small bowl, whisk together the mayonnaise, pickles, ketchup, horseradish, and pepper and set aside.

2 In a small saucepan, combine the broth and pickling spices and bring to a simmer over medium heat. Add the seitan, cover, reduce the heat to low, and cook for 10—40 minutes, the longer the better. Remove the seitan from the cooking liquid, brush off the spices, and cut it into ½-inch (12-mm) slices.

3 Place 4 slices of bread on a work surface. Put 1 slice of cheese on each piece of bread, followed by the seitan, sauerkraut, and another piece of cheese. Spoon 2 tablespoons of the dressing on the remaining pieces of bread and place them dressing-side down on top of the sandwiches.

4 In a large nonstick frying pan (or 2 pans if necessary to fit all the sandwiches), melt the butter over medium-low heat. Add the sandwiches and cook until the bread is toasted and the cheese has melted, about 3 minutes per side. Serve right away.

If you're short on time, substitute thin-sliced vegetarian deli meat (I like Tofurky brand Peppered Deli Slices) for the seitan, putting them directly on the sandwiches without simmering them in broth.

(V) The mild heat in this classic Chinese soup comes from white pepper instead of chiles. I like to serve this soup with warmed frozen vegetarian egg rolls for the full take-out meal experience.

# Hot-and-Sour Soup

**Dried shiitake mushrooms,** 4

**Dried cloud ear mushrooms** (optional), 2 tablespoons (¼ oz/7 g)

**Boiling water,** 4¼ cups (34 fl oz/ 1 l plus 60 ml)

**Vegetable bouillon cubes,** 2, or 4 teaspoons vegetarian broth powder

**Canned bamboo shoots,** ½ cup (2½ oz/75 g), cut into thin strips

**Soy sauce,** 3 tablespoons, plus more if desired

**Cornstarch,** 2 tablespoons

**Sugar,** ¾ teaspoon

**Snow peas,** 1 cup (6 oz/180 g), strings removed, thinly sliced

**Firm tofu,** ¼ lb (125 g), cut into thin strips

**Ground white pepper,** 1½ teaspoons

**Large eggs,** 2, beaten

**Chinese black vinegar or apple cider vinegar,** 3 tablespoons

**Green onions,** 2, chopped

**MAKES 4 SERVINGS**

1   In a large, heatproof bowl, place the shiitake and cloud ear mushrooms. Pour the boiling water over them; let stand for 30 minutes. Thinly slice the caps of the shiitake mushrooms, discarding the stems, and cut the cloud ear mushrooms into julienne strips. Set aside the mushrooms and soaking liquid.

2   Pour the soaking liquid into a saucepan, discarding the last few tablespoons of soaking liquid if they are gritty. Add the mushrooms, bouillon cubes, and bamboo shoots. Bring to a simmer over medium-high heat. Reduce the heat to low, cover, and cook for 5 minutes.

3   In a small bowl, pour the soy sauce over the cornstarch; add the sugar and whisk to dissolve. Add the mixture to the soup and bring to a simmer over medium-high heat; cook until thickened and bubbly, 2 minutes.

4   Reduce the heat to medium-low and stir in the snow peas, tofu, and white pepper. Pour the beaten eggs into the soup in a slow steady stream, and cook without stirring, until the egg strands turn opaque and rise to the surface, 1 minute. Gently stir in the vinegar. Season with additional soy sauce, if desired.

5   Divide the soup among bowls, sprinkle with the green onions, and serve right away.

It's key to use a mild vegetable bouillon broth (such as bouillon broth powder or cubes dissolved in hot water) in this recipe, as regular canned vegetable broth will obscure the delicate flavors of the soup.

✕

Chinese black vinegar, also called Chinkiang vinegar, is a robust-tasting rice vinegar that gives this soup the ideal bite. You can find it at Asian markets, but if you don't have one nearby, you can mix together equal parts red wine vinegar and balsamic vinegar.

(V) This warm, comforting stew is seasoned with a spice blend called *panch phoron* ("5 spices"), which gives the dish its authentic flavor. Serve with purchased naan bread or hot basmati rice and a little jarred chutney.

# Chickpea, Spinach, and Carrot Curry

**Canola oil,** 2 tablespoons

***Panch phoron* spice blend,** 2 teaspoons (see Note)

**Yellow onion,** ½, thinly sliced

**Large carrots,** 2, peeled and thinly sliced on the bias

**Fresh ginger,** 2 tablespoons finely chopped

**Garlic,** 1 tablespoon finely chopped

**Canned chopped tomatoes in sauce** (I like Pomi brand), 3 cups (26½ oz/ 750 g)

**Chickpeas,** 1 can (15 oz/425 g), rinsed and drained

**Baby spinach,** 2 cups (2 oz/60 g), loosely packed

**Sea salt and freshly ground pepper**

**MAKES 4 SERVINGS**

1 In a large sauté pan, warm the oil over medium heat. Add the *panch phoron* and sauté until the spices are aromatic, 1 minute. Add the onion and carrots and sauté until they begin to brown, 5 minutes. Add the ginger and garlic and sauté until aromatic, 1 minute.

2 Add the tomatoes and chickpeas and bring to a simmer. Cook, stirring occasionally, until the carrots are tender and the sauce has thickened a bit, 15 minutes. Add the spinach and simmer until wilted, 5 minutes.

3 Season the curry to taste with salt and pepper. Divide the curry among bowls and serve right away.

*Panch phoron* is a whole spice blend from Northeastern India that adds a beguiling flavor to any simmered tomato dish. Look for it at gourmet stores, Indian groceries, and online. Alternatively, you can make your own by blending equal parts nigella (black onion) seeds, fennel seeds, fenugreek seeds, brown mustard seeds, and cumin seeds. *Panch phoron* lasts in an airtight container in your pantry for up to 6 months.

Sweet, tender leeks, buttery artichoke hearts, and bloomy-rind cheese sing of the fresh flavors of spring. Serve with baby greens sprinkled with lemon juice, extra-virgin olive oil, and a pinch of flaky sea salt.

# Whole-Wheat Pizza with Melted Leeks and Artichokes

**Pizza Dough,** page 184

**Cornmeal,** for dusting

**Unsalted butter,** 1 tablespoon

**Leeks,** 3, white and light green parts only thinly sliced (about 3 cups/ 9 oz/280 g)

**Fresh thyme,** 1 tablespoon chopped

**Dry white wine,** 2 tablespoons

**Frozen artichoke hearts,** 1 cup (6 oz/185 g), thawed and drained

**Sea salt and freshly ground pepper**

**Bloomy-rind sheep's- or goat's-milk cheese** (such as Brebiou), ½ lb (250 g), rind discarded

**MAKES 4 SERVINGS**

If you don't have a stand mixer, you can also make the dough in a food processor fitted with the plastic dough blade.

✕

For a superquick meal, substitute 1 pound (500 g) of fresh pizza dough purchased from a natural or specialty foods market.

1 Preheat the oven to 425°F (220°C). Meanwhile, follow the instructions on page 184 to make the pizza dough.

2 Sprinkle a rimmed baking sheet with cornmeal. On a lightly floured work surface, roll the dough into an 8-by-12-inch (20-by-30-cm) rectangle or rough oval. Transfer the dough to the baking sheet, brush with olive oil, and bake until pale-golden and dry to the touch, 10 minutes.

3 In a large sauté pan over medium-low heat, melt the butter. Add the leeks and thyme and sauté until the leeks have "melted" into a soft mass without browning, about 8 minutes. Add the wine and cook until evaporated, 2 minutes. Add the artichokes and heat through, 2 minutes. Season with salt and pepper.

4 Spread the leek mixture over the prebaked crust. Distribute dabs of the cheese on top of the pizza and bake until the crust is golden-brown and the cheese is bubbly, 12—15 minutes. Cut into squares and serve.

Think of this as a springboard for other risottos: When in season, swap asparagus, zucchini, wild mushrooms, or butternut squash for the peas. In this version, roasted slices of Meyer lemon lend a sweet-tangy zip.

# Pea Risotto with Pea Shoots and Roasted Meyer Lemon

**Extra-virgin olive oil,** 2 teaspoons

**Small Meyer lemons,** 2, halved lengthwise and thinly sliced, seeds removed

**Vegetable broth,** 5 cups (40 fl oz/1.25 l)

**Unsalted butter,** 3 tablespoons

**Shallots,** 1 cup (5 oz/155 g) thinly sliced

**Arborio rice,** 1½ cups (10½ oz/330 g)

**Dry vermouth or dry white wine,** ½ cup (4 fl oz/125 ml)

**Fresh shelled peas,** 2 cups (10 oz/ 315 g) (from about 2 lb/1 kg pea pods)

**Young pecorino cheese,** 1 cup (4 oz/ 125 g) finely grated

**Sea salt and freshly ground pepper**

**Pea shoots,** 2 cups (2 oz/60 g), chopped if unruly

**MAKES 4 SERVINGS**

If you're pressed for time, look for shelled fresh peas at farmers' markets and in the produce department at gourmet grocery stores.

✄

I recommend pecorino cheese, a young, creamy sheep's-milk cheese, to complement the delicate flavors in this recipe; its aged cousin, pecorino romano, is much saltier. If you can't find young pecorino, Parmesan cheese makes a good substitute.

1 Preheat the oven to 400°F (200°C). Line a baking sheet with parchment paper and brush with some of the olive oil. Arrange the lemon slices in a single layer, drizzle with the remaining oil, and roast until lightly browned, 15 minutes. Chop the lemons and set aside.

2 Heat the broth in a small saucepan or in a large measuring cup in the microwave until steaming hot. Keep warm. In a heavy saucepan, melt the butter over medium heat. Add the shallots and sauté until tender but not browned, 3 minutes. Add the rice and cook, stirring constantly, 1 minute. Add the vermouth and cook until the liquid has been absorbed, 1 minute. Add about ½ cup (4 fl oz/125 ml) hot broth and simmer, stirring frequently, until the broth has been absorbed. Repeat with the remaining broth, adding only ½ cup of the broth at a time, until all the broth has been added and the rice is just tender, about 18 minutes. During the last 8 minutes of cooking, add the peas.

3 Remove the pot from the heat and stir in the cheese. Season to taste with salt and pepper. Divide the risotto among 4 shallow bowls. Sprinkle some of the roasted lemon on top of each portion. Garnish each bowl with a tangle of pea shoots and serve.

In this dressed-up version of a British classic, I ladle a lentil-based stew onto crisp slabs of whole-grain bread and add shaved aged Manchego cheese for a salty zing. Serve this with a big Nebbiolo from Northwestern Italy.

# Lentils, Kale, and Manchego on Garlic Toast

**Brown lentils,** 1½ cups (10 ½ oz/330 g)

**Shallots,** ½ cup (2 ¼ oz/75 g) finely chopped

**Carrot,** 1, peeled and chopped

**Celery stalk,** 1, chopped

**Dried bay leaf,** 1

**Sea salt,** ½ teaspoon

**Olive oil,** 2 tablespoons

**Fresh rosemary,** 2 teaspoons finely chopped

**Kale,** 4 cups chopped (4 oz/125 g), tough center stalks discarded

**Tomato sauce,** 1 cup (8 fl oz/250 ml)

**Vegetarian Worcestershire sauce,** 1 tablespoon

**Freshly ground pepper**

**Garlic,** 1 large clove, peeled

**Crusty sourdough bread,** 1 loaf (14 oz/440 g)

**Manchego cheese,** ⅓ cup (1 oz/30 g), shaved with a sharp vegetable peeler

**MAKES 4 SERVINGS**

1   In a saucepan, combine the lentils, shallots, carrot, celery, bay leaf, salt, and 5 cups (40 fl oz/1.25 l) water. Bring to a boil, reduce the heat to maintain a gentle simmer, cover, and cook until the lentils are tender, about 30 minutes.

2   While the lentils are simmering, sauté the kale. In a sauté pan, warm the oil and rosemary over medium heat. Add the kale and sauté, tossing with tongs, until the kale is wilted, 2 minutes. Add the kale mixture to the lentils. Stir in the tomato sauce and Worcestershire sauce. Bring the mixture to a simmer over low heat and cook uncovered, stirring frequently, until the sauce has thickened, 10 minutes. Season with pepper and keep warm.

3   Place a rack in the top third of the oven and preheat the broiler. Rub the garlic all over the bread, then cut the loaf into ½-inch (12-mm) slices. Arrange the bread slices on a rimmed baking sheet in one layer and broil until lightly toasted, 2 minutes per side.

4   Divide the toast among 4 dinner plates. Spoon the lentil-kale mixture over the toasts and sprinkle with the cheese.

There's a long tradition of beans on toast as a quick supper in Great Britain, where it's called "thousand on a raft."

✖

You can use any type of kale for this recipe, such as Russian kale, dinosaur kale, or even curly kale.

✖

Make this dish really quick by substituting canned lentils or cannellini beans for the dried lentils and skip the shallots, carrot, and celery. Add the canned lentils/beans to the sautéed kale along with the tomato sauce and Worcestershire sauce.

The combination of smoky morel mushrooms and asparagus gives this creamy lasagna a sophisticated flavor. No-boil lasagna noodles and a light cream sauce make it a breeze to make, even on a weeknight.

# Lasagna with Asparagus and Morel Mushrooms

If you can't find fresh morels, substitute ½ ounce (15 g) dried morels soaked in hot water for 30 minutes. Drain and chop before using.

✕

Leeks tend to be gritty. To wash them efficiently, cut them in half lengthwise and rinse under cold running water while bending them a bit to allow water to flush out any soil and grit trapped between the layers.

**Olive oil,** 1 tablespoon

**Leek,** 1, white and light green parts only, thinly sliced (about 1 cup/3 oz/ 90 g)

**Asparagus,** 1 lb (500 g), tough ends snapped off and stalks cut into 2-inch (5-cm) pieces

**Fresh morel mushrooms,** ¼ lb (125 g), roughly chopped

**Fresh rosemary,** 1 tablespoon chopped

**Sea salt and freshly ground pepper**

**Heavy cream,** 2 cups (16 fl oz/500 ml)

**Vegetable broth,** 1½ cups (12 fl oz/ 375 ml)

**Garlic,** 1 clove, lightly smashed with the side of a chef's knife

**Lemon juice,** 2 teaspoons

**Freshly grated nutmeg,** ¾ teaspoon

**No-boil lasagna sheets,** 6

**Parmesan cheese,** 1 cup (4 oz/125 g) finely grated

**MAKES 4 SERVINGS**

1 Preheat the oven to 350°F (180°C). Spray an 8-inch (20-cm) square baking dish with cooking spray. In a large sauté pan, warm the oil over medium heat. Add the leek and sauté until tender, 4 minutes. Add the asparagus, mushrooms, and rosemary. Sprinkle lightly with salt and pepper and sauté until the asparagus is bright green and tender-crisp, 4 minutes. Transfer the vegetables to a bowl and set aside.

2 Return the pan to the heat and add the cream, broth, and garlic. Bring to a simmer and cook for 5 minutes to reduce a bit (you should have 2½ cups/ 20 fl oz/625 ml liquid). Remove the pan from the heat, stir in the lemon juice and nutmeg, and discard the garlic clove. Season to taste with salt.

3 Spoon ½ cup (4 fl oz/125 ml) of the cream mixture into the baking dish, and arrange 2 pasta sheets on top. Spoon one-third of the asparagus mixture over the pasta, sprinkle with one-third of the cheese, and top with ½ cup more sauce. Repeat with two more layers of pasta, vegetables, sauce, and cheese. Cover the baking dish with foil and bake for 40 minutes. Uncover and bake until the cheese is golden-brown, 6—8 minutes. Let the lasagna stand at room temperature for 5 minutes before serving.

# Summer

# Summer

Summer's bounty makes cooking easy and relaxed. It's the time for al fresco dinners inspired by your farmer's market haul, creative meatless takes on hot dogs and burgers, and delicious foods from warm-weather cuisines, like Middle Eastern grilled stuffed eggplant with cooling cucumber yogurt sauce, spicy Thai noodles with crunchy vegetables, and juicy tomato-and-avocado-centric Mexican fare.

## Smart Strategies for Summer Cooking

- If you've got an outdoor grill, clean it thoroughly at the beginning of the season. Disassemble the grates, thoroughly clean out the bottom with a stiff wire brush, and clean with eco-friendly grill cleaner.

- Avocados are a natural for summer food, adding richness without cooking a thing. Keep a few unripe ones on the windowsill and use them as they ripen.

- Heirloom tomatoes are a summer treasure, but they can be expensive, so handle them with care. Never store tomatoes in the refrigerator or they will go from juicy to mealy in no time.

- Basil goes with almost all summer produce, especially eggplant, tomatoes, and zucchini. It's easy to grow in pots or in the garden. I like to plant several different types, including spicy Thai, sweet Genovese, and zesty cinnamon basil. Tear the leaves and toss them in salads and add them as a fresh garnish at the last minute to everything else.

- Stone fruit and berries make amazing desserts. Serve sliced white peaches in goblets with Italian sparkling wine, layer berries with sweetened whipped cream and store-bought meringue cookies, or try grilling halved peaches and serving them with pistachio ice cream.

## Super-Simple Summer Sides

- Get creative with grilled sweet corn. Rub grilled ears with lime juice and sprinkle with garam masala, or coat with equal parts butter and white miso and sprinkle with Japanese furikake (nori and sesame condiment). Alternatively, try corn Italian-style with a topping of soft butter, finely grated Parmigiano-Reggiano cheese, and truffle salt.

- Toss padrón or shishito peppers with olive oil, grill them until lightly charred, and sprinkle with crunchy sea salt. These are also great as a quick appetizer or cocktail-party fare.

- For a quick ratatouille, grill cherry tomatoes, thinly sliced bell peppers, and diced zucchini in a grill basket. Add torn fresh basil, olive oil, and a splash of vinegar and toss together gently.

- For a refreshing salad, toss watermelon chunks with thinly sliced jalapeño peppers, creamy feta-cheese crumbles, and finely chopped fresh cilantro.

- Roll out purchased fresh pizza dough into thin rounds, brush with olive oil, and grill until puffed and lightly charred. Serve with hummus, olives, and sliced cucumbers.

This easy but satisfying pasta dish helps use up a glut of summer squash and tomatoes in late summer. Arugula adds a peppery bite to counter the richness of the cheese-stuffed pasta, but spinach would also be tasty.

# Cheese Tortellini with Roasted Vegetables and Arugula

This recipes doubles as a wonderful pasta salad: Rinse the cooked tortellini with cold water to stop them from cooking and proceed with the recipe, omitting the ½ cup (4 fl oz/125 ml) cooking water added to the pasta at the end. Refrigerate for 1 hour or up to 2 days before serving, and add additional olive oil and red wine vinegar to taste before serving.

✖

For a more herbal quality, substitute 1 cup (1 oz/30 g) of torn fresh basil leaves for the arugula.

**Baby pattypan squash or zucchini,** 1 lb (500 g), cut into 1-inch (2.5-cm) chunks

**Cherry tomatoes or roughly chopped tomatoes,** 1 pint (12 oz/375 g)

**Pitted Kalamata olives,** ½ cup (2 oz/60 g)

**Garlic,** 8 cloves, unpeeled

**Olive oil,** 2 tablespoons

**Sea salt and freshly ground pepper**

**Fresh cheese or spinach tortellini,** 1¼ lb (625 g)

**Parmesan cheese,** ⅓ cup (1⅓ oz/ 40 g) grated

**Arugula leaves,** 4 cups (4 oz/125 g) loosely packed, roughly chopped if large

**MAKES 4—6 SERVINGS**

1 Preheat the oven to 400°F (200°C). Line a rimmed baking sheet with parchment paper. Toss the squash, tomatoes, olives, garlic, and oil on the baking sheet until coated. Sprinkle with salt and pepper and roast until the squash is tender and the cherry tomatoes fall apart, 30 minutes.

2 While the vegetables roast, bring a large pot of salted water to a boil. Ten minutes before the vegetables are done, boil the tortellini according to the package instructions.

3 Remove the skins from the garlic, then mash the garlic with a fork. Reserve ½ cup (4 fl oz/125 ml) of the cooking water, then drain the pasta. Stir the mashed garlic into the reserved cooking water.

4 In a large serving bowl, combine the tortellini with the roasted vegetables, garlic flavored cooking water, and cheese and toss to coat. Add the arugula and toss once more to combine and gently wilt the arugula. Season to taste with salt and pepper, and serve right away.

This is the perfect answer to a pizza craving on a hot day when you'd rather not turn on the oven. With grilled onions, heirloom tomatoes, and peppery arugula mounded on top, this pizza is summer on a plate.

# Summer Vegetable Grilled Pizza

**Garlic,** 1 small clove, chopped and smashed with the side of a chef's knife

**Extra-virgin olive oil,** ¼ cup (2 fl oz/60 ml)

**Arugula,** 5 oz (155 g), torn

**Fennel,** ½ cup (1½ oz/45 g) shaved

**Lemon juice,** 1 tablespoon

**Truffle salt**

**Freshly ground pepper**

**Sweet onion,** 1, halved lengthwise and thinly sliced

**Pizza dough,** homemade (page 184) or purchased, 1 lb (450 g), at room temperature

**Heirloom tomatoes,** 2, sliced

**Fresh mozzarella cheese,** ½ lb (250 g), thinly sliced

**Parmesan cheese,** ⅓ cup (1⅓ oz/40 g) grated

**MAKES 4 SERVINGS**

1 Set up a grill for indirect-heat cooking over medium heat. Meanwhile, in a small bowl, mix the garlic with 2 tablespoons of the oil and set aside. In a large bowl, toss the arugula and fennel with 1 tablespoon of the oil, the lemon juice, and a pinch each of truffle salt and pepper; set aside.

2 Toss the onion with the remaining 1 tablespoon oil. Place a perforated grill pan on the hot side of the grill, add the onion, and cook until the onion is softened and lightly charred, 6 minutes. Remove from the grill.

3 Divide the pizza dough into 2 equal pieces. On a lightly floured surface, roll each piece into an 11-inch (28-cm) round. Stack the rounds between sheets of parchment paper and transfer to a baking sheet. Transfer the rounds from the baking sheet directly to the hot side of the grill, discarding the paper. Cover the grill and cook until the bottoms are lightly browned, 3 minutes. Flip and grill until the second side is browned and crisp, 4 minutes.

4 Move the rounds to the cool side of the grill and brush the tops with the garlic oil. Quickly divide the reserved grilled onion, tomato, and cheeses on the pizza rounds. Sprinkle with truffle salt and pepper. Cover and cook until the cheese has melted, 5—8 minutes. Slide the pizzas to the hot part of the grill and cook for a few moments to crisp up the bottoms. If you like, cut the pizzas in half and top with the arugula salad. Serve right away.

To set up a gas grill for indirect heat, turn on just one burner, leaving the second one off. If using a charcoal grill, prepare the grill with a hot side and a "cool zone" where there are no coals. Allow the coals to ash over before proceeding.

✕

If the dough springs back while rolling it out, let it rest for 5 minutes.

(V) In Mexico, these small masa cakes are often filled with shredded meat. Here, I stuff them with refried beans, salsa, and avocado. Though they are vegan and petite, they're actually quite filling—three sopes make a meal.

# Black Bean–Avocado Sopes

**Masa Dough,** page 184

**Extra-virgin olive oil,** 1 tablespoon

**Yellow onion,** 1⅓ cups (7 oz/220 g) finely chopped

**Cumin seeds,** 1½ teaspoons

**Black beans,** 2 cans (15 oz/425 g), drained and rinsed

**Tomatoes,** 2 cups (12 oz/375 g) diced

**Fresh cilantro,** ½ cup (⅔ oz/20 g) finely chopped

**Jalapeño chile,** 1, finely chopped

**Lime juice,** 1 tablespoon

**Canola oil,** 1½ cups (12 fl oz/375 ml)

**Romaine lettuce,** 2 cups (2 oz/60 g) finely shredded

**Small ripe avocados,** 2, halved, pitted, peeled, and cut into cubes

**MAKES 4 SERVINGS**

If you're short on time, you can use purchased refried black beans and jarred salsa instead of making your own.

✂

If you don't have a deep cast-iron pan, you can use a heavy deep saucepan to fry the sopes.

✂

If the masa dough seems too crumbly as you are forming the sopes, knead a few drops of water into the dough.

1 Preheat the oven to 200°F (95°C). Meanwhile, follow the instructions on page 184 to make the dough for the sope shells and shape it into balls.

2 In a saucepan, warm the olive oil over medium-high heat. Add 1 cup (5 oz/155 g) of the onion and the cumin seeds and sauté until they begin to brown, 2½ minutes. Add the beans and mash with a potato masher until nearly smooth. Add 1 cup (8 fl oz/250 ml) water and bring to a simmer. Reduce the heat to low and keep warm. In a bowl, combine the remaining ⅓ cup (2 oz/45 g) onion, the tomatoes, cilantro, jalapeño, and lime juice. Season the beans and the tomato mixture to taste with salt.

3 In a deep cast iron pan, warm the canola oil over medium-high heat until it reaches 350°F (180°C) on a deep-frying thermometer. Meanwhile, press the masa balls between your palms and then transfer them to a sheet of plastic wrap. Pat them out with your fingertips until they are about 3 inches (7.5 cm) in diameter. Pinch up the edges to form little tart shells. Cover the completed shells with plastic wrap as you work. When the oil is ready, fry the sopes in batches of three until golden brown and crisp, 2—3 minutes. Transfer the fried sopes to a baking sheet and keep them warm in the oven while frying the remaining ones.

4 Divide the bean mixture among the masa shells. Top with the tomato mixture, lettuce, and avocado.

Called bibimbap, which means "mixed rice" in Korean, this dish uses short-grain rice as a stage for colorful mounds of blanched vegetables and kimchi. A fried egg on top of each bowl provides protein and richness.

# Korean Vegetable-Rice Bowls

**Large cucumber,** 1, halved lengthwise and seeded

**Sea salt**

**Toasted sesame oil and rice vinegar,** 2 teaspoons *each*

**Sesame seeds,** 2 teaspoons, toasted

**Large carrots,** 2, peeled and cut into matchsticks

**Baby spinach,** 10 oz (315 g)

**Soy sauce,** 2 teaspoons

**Canola oil,** 1½ teaspoons

**Large eggs,** 4

**Warm steamed short-grain rice,** such as CalRose, 8 cups (40 oz/1.25 kg)

**Bean sprouts,** 2 cups (2 oz/60 g)

**Nori seaweed,** 1 sheet, cut with scissors into thin strips

**Napa cabbage kimchi,** 1¼ cups (5 oz/155 g)

**Gochujang or Sriracha sauce,** for serving

**MAKES 4 SERVINGS**

When making short-grain rice, count on the fact that it triples in volume when cooked. For the amount of rice called for here, start with 2⅔ cups (18¾ oz/580 g) uncooked rice.

Gochujang is a sweet-hot red chile condiment available at Asian markets and increasingly available at some grocery stores. It keeps indefinitely in the refrigerator and is delicious on everything from tacos to hot dogs.

1  Cut the cucumber halves crosswise into ⅛-inch (12-mm) slices and place in a colander. Toss with 1 teaspoon salt and set aside for 10 minutes. Rinse the cucumbers well, gather them in a clean dish towel, and squeeze to extract as much liquid as possible. Transfer to a small bowl and toss with 1 teaspoon of the sesame oil, 1½ teaspoons of the vinegar, and 1 teaspoon of the sesame seeds; set aside.

2  Bring a large pot of water to a boil. Add the carrots and cook until just tender, 1 minute. Using a slotted spoon, remove the carrots from the water, rinse with cold water, drain, and transfer to a bowl. Toss with the remaining ½ teaspoon vinegar and ¼ teaspoon salt. Repeat the process cooking with the spinach, cooking until the leaves are just wilted, 1 minute. Squeeze all the liquid from the leaves, place them in a bowl, and toss with the remaining 1 teaspoon sesame oil, 1 teaspoon sesame seeds, and the soy sauce.

3  Warm a large nonstick frying pan over medium heat. Add the oil and crack the eggs into the pan, spacing them evenly. Fry until the whites are set and the yolks are still runny, 3—5 minutes.

4  Divide the rice among 4 large bowls. Place small mounds of the cucumber, carrots, spinach, and sprouts around the rice. Place an egg in the center of each bowl. Sprinkle with the nori strips. Pass the kimchi and gochujang.

(V) This is my version of the peanutty sesame noodles at Cantonese restaurants far and wide. Since these are filling but refreshingly cold, they're the ideal picnic or potluck dish on warm summer evenings.

# Sesame Noodles with Green Beans and Tofu

**FOR THE SAUCE**

**Creamy all-natural peanut butter,** ⅓ cup (3 oz/90 g)

**Brewed green tea,** ½ cup (4 fl oz/ 125 ml), warmed

**Soy sauce,** ¼ cup (2 fl oz/60 ml)

**Apple cider vinegar,** 2 tablespoons

**Fresh ginger,** 1 tablespoon minced

**Garlic,** 2 teaspoons finely chopped

**Brown sugar,** 1 tablespoon firmly packed

**Dark sesame oil,** 2 teaspoons

**Asian chile oil,** 2 teaspoons (optional)

**FOR THE NOODLES**

**Linguini or spaghetti,** ¾ lb (375 g)

**Green beans,** ½ lb (250 g), trimmed and cut into 2-inch (5-cm) pieces

**Baked tofu,** 6 oz (185 g), cut into ¼-inch (6-mm) strips

**Red bell pepper,** ½, seeded and thinly sliced

**Celery,** 2 stalks, thinly sliced

**Large carrot,** 1, thinly sliced

**Toasted sesame seeds,** 3 tablespoons

**MAKES 4—6 SERVINGS**

This salad is great when made ahead, but the noodles will soak up the dressing. To serve any leftovers, add an additional ¼ cup (2 fl oz/60 ml) or so of warm green tea to re-moisten.

✕

The vegetables in this recipe are just a suggestion—you can use whatever you have on hand; you'll need 4 cups (32 fl oz/1 l) total of sliced vegetables by volume.

1 To make the sauce, in a bowl, combine the peanut butter, green tea, soy sauce, vinegar, ginger, garlic, brown sugar, sesame oil, and chile oil, if using. Whisk until smooth and set aside.

2 Bring a large pot of salted water to a boil. Add the pasta and cook according to the package instructions. During the last 2 minutes of cooking, add the green beans. Drain the pasta and beans and rinse thoroughly with cold water to cool. Drain well.

3 In a large serving bowl, place the pasta, green beans, tofu, bell pepper, celery, carrot, and sesame seeds. Pour the sauce over the noodles, toss to coat the ingredients well, and serve.

This is similar to the Italian comfort food dish, but it's infinitely easier: The eggplant is broiled instead of breaded and fried, and the sauce is jarred. A layer of Parmesan bread crumbs on top lends a crisp element.

# Skillet Eggplant Parmesan

**Globe eggplant,** 1 (1¼ lb/625 g), cut into ½-inch (12-mm) slices

**Extra-virgin olive oil,** ¼ cup (2 fl oz/ 60 ml)

**Sea salt and freshly ground pepper**

**Marinara sauce,** 1 jar (24 oz/750 g)

**Mozzarella cheese,** 1 cup (4 oz/125 g) shredded

**Fresh bread crumbs,** 1½ cups (3 oz/90 g)

**Parmesan cheese,** ½ cup (2 oz/60 g) grated

**Unsalted butter,** 2 tablespoons, melted

**Dried oregano,** 1½ teaspoons

**Garlic powder,** 1 teaspoon

**Spaghetti or capellini,** ½ lb (250 g)

**MAKES 4 SERVINGS**

For best results, don't substitute dried bread crumbs in this recipe. To make fresh bread crumbs, tear a roll or a few slices of bread into pieces and pulse in a food processor until you have fine crumbs. Fresh bread crumbs will keep in a sealable plastic bag in the freezer for up to 3 months.

1 Place a rack in the top third of the oven and preheat the broiler. Line a baking sheet with foil and spray with cooking spray. Place the eggplant in a single layer on the baking sheet, brush liberally with the oil, and sprinkle with salt and pepper. Broil until the eggplant is browned and fork-tender, 4 minutes per side. Set the eggplant aside and reduce the oven heat to 425°F (220°C).

2 In a 14-inch (35-cm) ovenproof frying pan, warm the marinara sauce over medium heat until simmering. Arrange the eggplant slices evenly, overlapping, on top of the sauce, and sprinkle the mozzarella on top.

3 In a small bowl, combine the bread crumbs, Parmesan, butter, oregano, and garlic powder and mix well. Sprinkle the bread crumb mixture evenly over the ingredients in the frying pan. Place the pan in the oven and bake until the sauce is bubbly and the crumbs are golden-brown, 15 minutes.

4 While the eggplant bakes, cook the spaghetti according to package instructions. Serve with the eggplant and sauce.

Pad Kee Mao, literally "drunken noodles" in Thai, is an addictive street food featuring wide noodles, spicy sauce, vegetables, and basil. This version is tame by Thai standards, so I pass chile sauce at the table.

# Spicy Thai Noodles with Vegetables and Basil

**Wide rice noodles,** ½ lb (250 g), about ½-inch (12-mm) wide

**Sriracha sauce,** 2 tablespoons, plus more to taste

**Mushroom soy sauce,** 3 tablespoons

**Sugar,** 2 teaspoons

**Vegetable oil,** 2 tablespoons

**Shallots,** ¼ cup (1 oz/30 g) thinly sliced

**Garlic,** 1 tablespoon finely chopped

**Broccoli florets,** 1½ cups (3 oz/90 g), cut into bite-size pieces

**Tomatoes,** ¾ cup (4½ oz/140 g) chopped

**Carrot,** ½ cup (2 oz/60 g) thinly sliced

**Large eggs,** 3, lightly beaten

**Bean sprouts,** 1 cup (1 oz/30 g)

**Fresh basil leaves,** ⅔ cup (⅔ oz/20 g) loosely packed, torn

**Fresh cilantro leaves,** ½ cup (⅔ oz/20 g) chopped

**Toasted peanuts,** ¼ cup (1¼ oz/35 g), chopped

**Lime,** 1, cut into 6 wedges

**MAKES 4 SERVINGS**

Thai food relies heavily on fish sauce for seasoning. When cooking for vegetarians, I rely on mushroom soy sauce for that rich, salty flavor. Look for it at Asian markets or online. If you are not a strict vegetarian, use 2 tablespoons of Asian fish sauce instead of the soy sauce for a more authentic flavor.

When shopping for rice noodles, look for noodles labeled "bahn pho" at Asian markets or with other Asian foods at well-stocked supermarkets.

1  Bring 2 quarts (2 l) water to a boil. Place the noodles in a large, heatproof bowl. Pour the boiling water over the noodles and let soak until pliable, 15 minutes. Drain, rinse with cold water, and set aside. In a small bowl, combine the Sriracha, soy sauce, and sugar, and set aside.

2  In a wok or large, deep sauté pan, warm 1 tablespoon of the oil over medium-high heat. Add the shallots and stir-fry until they begin to turn golden brown, 2 minutes. Add the garlic and stir-fry for 10 seconds. Add the broccoli, tomatoes, and carrot, and stir-fry until the tomatoes fall apart and the broccoli is tender-crisp and bright-green, 3 minutes. Push the vegetables to one side of the wok; add the eggs and cook, stirring with a spatula, until the eggs are just set, 1 minute. Scrape the contents of the wok into a bowl.

3  Return the wok to medium-high heat and add the remaining 1 tablespoon oil. Add the noodles and let cook without stirring for 30 seconds, then stir-fry until lightly charred and warmed through, 1 minute. Add the vegetable-egg mixture, Sriracha mixture, sprouts, basil, and cilantro, and toss gently. Sprinkle the noodles with peanuts and serve with lime wedges on the side.

This warm salad is a sophisticated take on the classic three-bean salad. It features crisp green beans, tender cannellini beans, and warm haloumi, a firm Mediterranean cheese. Serve with a crusty baguette.

# Summer Bean Salad with Fried Haloumi and Pesto

**Fresh basil leaves,** 2 cups (2 oz/60 g)

**Extra-virgin olive oil,** ½ cup (4 fl oz/ 125 ml) plus 2 teaspoons

**Lemon juice,** 1 tablespoon

**Garlic,** 1 clove

**Sea salt and freshly ground pepper**

**Green beans,** ½ lb (250 g), trimmed

**Cannellini beans,** 1 can (15 oz/425 g), drained and rinsed

**Roasted red peppers,** 1 cup (6 oz/185 g), sliced

**Haloumi,** ½ lb (250 g), cut into 12 slices

**MAKES 4 SERVINGS**

If you're short on time, use quality purchased pesto instead of making your own. Be sure to check the label to make sure that fresh basil is one of the first ingredients listed.

1 To make the pesto, in a blender or food processor, combine the basil, ½ cup (4 fl oz/125 ml) of the oil, the lemon juice, and garlic. Blend until smooth. Season the pesto to taste with salt and pepper.

2 Bring a saucepan of water to a boil. Add the green beans and cook until tender-crisp, 4 minutes. Drain and toss with the cannellini beans and red peppers in a large bowl. Season with salt and pepper to taste.

3 In a large nonstick frying pan, warm the remaining 2 teaspoons oil over medium-high heat. Add the haloumi slices in a single layer and cook until browned, 1½ minutes per side.

4 Transfer the bean salad to a platter. Arrange the haloumi on a platter and drizzle with the pesto. (Alternatively, divide the salad among 4 plates. Top with the haloumi and drizzle the pesto over the top). Serve right away.

I'm crazy for dishes that combine textures. These tacos feature crunchy corn shells filled with zesty pinto beans and crisp vegetables. The crispy tacos are then tucked into soft flour tortillas smeared with spicy guacamole.

# Two-Layer Tacos with Pinto Beans and Guacamole

**Fresh cilantro leaves,** ¼ cup (¼ oz/7 g)

**Green onions,** 2, sliced

**Serrano chile,** 1, sliced

**Sea salt**

**Ripe avocados,** 2

**Lime juice,** 1 tablespoon

**Extra-virgin olive oil,** 1 tablespoon

**Garlic,** 2 teaspoons finely chopped

**Pinto beans,** 2 cans (15 oz/425 g), drained and rinsed

**Mexican oregano,** 1½ teaspoons

**Flour tortillas** (8 inches/20 cm), 8, warmed

**Crisp corn taco shells,** 8

**Pepper jack or Cheddar cheese,** 1 cup (4 oz/125 g) shredded

**Romaine lettuce,** 3 cups (3 oz/90 g) shredded

**Large ripe tomato,** 1, chopped

**Hot-pepper sauce**

**MAKES 4 SERVINGS**

Available from Latino groceries and some supermarkets, Mexican oregano has an earthy flavor that's worth seeking out, especially if you love Mexican food. However, standard oregano will also work in a pinch.

1 To make the guacamole, mound the cilantro, green onion, and serrano chile on a cutting board. Sprinkle 2 pinches of salt over the mound and chop until the mixture is finely minced. Cut open the avocados, remove the pits, and use a large spoon to scoop the flesh into a bowl. Add the cilantro mixture and lime juice and mash with a fork until mostly smooth; set aside.

2 In a saucepan, warm the oil over medium heat. Add the garlic and sauté until aromatic, 30 seconds. Add the pinto beans and oregano and cook, stirring frequently, until the beans begin to brown, 5 minutes. Add ½ cup (4 fl oz/125 ml) water, reduce the heat, and continue to simmer, stirring frequently, while you prepare the remaining ingredients.

3 Spread the guacamole evenly among the flour tortillas. Place a hard taco shell in the center of each flour tortilla. Season the beans to taste with salt. Fill the corn tortillas with the pinto beans, cheese, lettuce, and tomato, dividing evenly. Bring the sides of the flour tortillas up around the crisp tortillas and press them to adhere to the sides. Serve, passing the hot sauce at the table.

This Southwestern-style frittata offers zing from the chiles, moistness from the zucchini, and creaminess from the soft cheese. Serve with a jicama and melon salad sprinkled with New Mexican chile powder.

# Zucchini, Poblano, and Goat Cheese Frittata

**Large eggs,** 8

**Fresh cilantro,** 3 tablespoons finely chopped

**Sea salt and freshly ground pepper**

**Extra-virgin olive oil,** 1 tablespoon

**Small poblano chile,** 1, seeded and thinly sliced

**Green onions,** 2, thinly sliced

**Zucchini,** 1 cup (5 oz/155 g), shredded on the large holes of a box grater/ shredder

**Fresh goat cheese,** ¼ cup (2 oz/60 g)

**MAKES 4 SERVINGS**

Frittatas are endlessly adaptable. For a Mediterranean approach, use basil and roasted red pepper instead of cilantro and poblano chile. For an American-style meal, try it with chives, blanched broccoli, and Cheddar cheese.

1 Place a rack in the top third of the oven and preheat the broiler. In a bowl, whisk together the eggs and cilantro with ½ teaspoon each salt and pepper.

2 Spray a 10-inch (25-cm) ovenproof nonstick frying pan with cooking spray. Add the oil to the pan and warm over medium-high heat. Add the chile and green onions and sauté until tender, 3 minutes. Add the zucchini and sauté until tender and wilted, 2 minutes.

3 Reduce the heat to low and pour the egg mixture into the frying pan. Distribute dabs of the cheese evenly on top. Cover and cook until the edges set up and the center is just set, 10 minutes. Remove the lid, place the pan under the broiler, and broil until the top is lightly browned and puffed, 4 minutes. Remove the frittata from the oven and let it stand for 5 minutes.

4 To serve, slide a rubber spatula under the edges to loosen the frittata and transfer it to a large plate. Cut into wedges and serve right away.

(V) This style of curry does not include coconut milk, as it comes from the northern part of Thailand where coconuts don't grow. If you're not a strict vegetarian, use Asian fish sauce in place of mushroom soy sauce.

# Northern Thai–Style Curry with Tofu

**Vegetable broth,** ¾ cup (6 fl oz/180 ml)

**Mushroom soy sauce,** 2 tablespoons

**Lime juice,** 1 tablespoon

**Brown sugar,** 2 teaspoons firmly packed

**Canola oil,** 2 tablespoons

**Firm tofu,** 10 oz (315 g), cut into ½-inch (12-mm) cubes

**Green curry paste,** 3 tablespoons

**Baby corn,** 1 cup (6 oz/185 g), cut into ½-inch (12-mm) lengths

**Japanese eggplant,** 1, cut into ½-inch (12-mm) cubes

**Small red bell pepper,** 1, seeded and sliced

**Green beans,** ¼ lb (125 g), trimmed and cut into 2-inch (5-cm) lengths

**Dried lime leaves** (optional), 12

**Fresh basil leaves,** 1 cup (1 oz/30 g), roughly chopped or torn

**Steamed jasmine rice or quinoa,** for serving

**MAKES 4 SERVINGS**

1 In a glass measuring cup, mix together the broth, soy sauce, lime juice, and brown sugar; set aside.

2 In a wok or large, deep sauté pan, warm 1 tablespoon of the oil over medium-high heat. Add the tofu and stir-fry until browned, 3 minutes. Transfer the tofu to a bowl and set aside.

3 Reduce the heat to medium and add the remaining 1 tablespoon oil. Add the curry paste and cook, stirring constantly, until aromatic, 20 seconds. Add the baby corn, eggplant, bell pepper, green beans, and lime leaves, if using, and stir-fry until the vegetables are fork tender, 5–8 minutes.

4 Reduce the heat to medium-low and add the tofu and broth mixture. Toss gently to combine and simmer, stirring occasionally, until the eggplant is very tender when pierced with a fork, about 5 minutes. Gently fold in the basil and serve right away with the rice.

To ensure your dish is truly vegetarian, check the label before buying Thai curry paste, as some contain dried shrimp.

✕

Sold at Asian markets, dried lime leaves add a floral, herbal flavor to stir-fries and soups, and freeze well for up to three months. Like dried bay leaves, they are too tough to eat whole. Either remove them before serving or warn diners that they are not to be eaten.

✕

Generally these curries are very spicy, but this version is only moderately hot. Feel free to add more curry paste if you prefer something more fiery.

This protein-packed dish is reminiscent of an old-school taco casserole, but instead of ground beef and rice, I use seitan and red quinoa. The result is a quick meal that satisfies Mexican food cravings in a healthy way.

# Mexican Quinoa and Vegetable Casserole

**Red quinoa,** ¾ cup (6 oz/185 g)

**Sea salt and freshly ground pepper**

**Olive oil,** 2 tablespoons

**Yellow onion,** 1 cup (5 oz/155 g) finely chopped

**Small red bell pepper,** 1, chopped

**Frozen corn,** 1 cup (6 oz/185 g)

**Seitan,** ½ lb (250 g), chopped or crumbled

**Chili powder,** 1 tablespoon

**Black beans,** 1 can (15 oz/425 g), drained and rinsed

**Jarred tomato salsa,** ½ cup (4 fl oz/125 ml)

**Pepper jack cheese,** 1 cup (4 oz/125 g) shredded

**Fresh cilantro** (optional), ½ cup (¾ oz/20 g) chopped

**MAKES 4 SERVINGS**

1 In a small saucepan, bring 1¼ cups (10 fl oz/310 ml) water to a boil. Add the quinoa and ½ teaspoon salt, reduce the heat to medium-low, cover, and cook until tender, 15 minutes.

2 In a large ovenproof frying pan, warm the oil over medium-high heat. Add the onion, bell pepper, corn, seitan, and chili powder and cook until the vegetables are tender, 5 minutes. Reduce the heat to low and fold in the beans and salsa; cook 1 minute. Remove the pan from the heat and gently fold in the quinoa. Season to taste with salt and pepper.

3 Place a rack in the top third of the oven and preheat the broiler. Sprinkle the quinoa mixture evenly with the cheese. Broil until the cheese is melted and bubbly, 5 minutes. Sprinkle with the cilantro and serve.

Save a step and buy a packet of precooked quinoa, available in shelf-stable bags and in the freezer department of grocery stores. You will need about 2 cups (12 oz/375 g) cooked quinoa for this recipe.

This cornmeal dough is easy to work with and ideal for making a freeform tart packed with summer's best flavors: ripe tomatoes, creamy mozzarella, and fresh basil. Serve with a chilled rosé and a simple green salad.

# Heirloom Tomato, Mozzarella, and Basil Galette

**Whole Wheat Galette Dough,** page 184

**Parmesan cheese,** ⅓ cup (1⅓ oz/40 g) grated

**Ripe tomatoes,** preferably heirloom, ½ lb (250 g), sliced and patted dry

**Fresh mozzarella,** ⅓ lb (155 g), thinly sliced

**Fresh basil leaves,** ½ cup (½ oz/15 g), torn into bite-size pieces

**Sea salt and freshly ground pepper**

**Large egg,** 1

**Truffle oil** (optional)

**MAKES 8 SLICES**

1  Preheat the oven to 425°F (220°C). Line a large rimmed baking sheet with parchment paper. Meanwhile, make the galette dough according to the instructions on page 184.

2  On a lightly floured surface, roll out the dough until it is 12 inches (30 cm) in diameter. Carefully transfer it to the prepared baking sheet. Sprinkle the Parmesan on the dough, leaving a 1½-inch (4-cm) border around the edge. Arrange the tomatoes on top of the Parmesan without overlapping. Top with the mozzarella and basil and season with salt and pepper. Fold the dough over the edges of the filling, letting it overlap here and there and pressing it together with your fingers if there are any tears.

3  In a small bowl, whisk the egg with 1 tablespoon water; brush the egg mixture over the dough. Bake until the crust is golden-brown on the bottom, 25 minutes.

4  Just before serving, drizzle the tart with the truffle oil, if using, and cut the tart into 8 wedges.

Vary the vegetables according to what is in season. I love grilled eggplant and peppers in summer, but this galette is equally lovely stuffed with sautéed greens and caramelized onions or roasted root vegetables.

✂

If you don't want to go to the trouble of getting out your food processor, you can make the dough for this galette by hand: whisk together the dry ingredients, then cut in the butter with a pastry blender. Stir in the buttermilk with a rubber spatula.

To reduce the amount of fat found in typical Chinese-style eggplant dishes, I first steam eggplant slices and then stir-fry them with a spicy sauce and just a splash of oil. Serve with rice and a cooling cucumber salad.

# Sichuan-Style Eggplant with Tofu

**Japanese eggplant,** 1 lb (500 g), cut on an angle into ½-inch (12-mm) slices

**Black bean–garlic sauce,** 1 tablespoon

**Chinese rice wine or dry sherry,** 1 tablespoon

**Soy sauce,** 1 tablespoon

**Sriracha or other chile sauce,** 1 tablespoon

**Chinese black vinegar or balsamic vinegar,** 2 teaspoons

**Sugar,** 1 teaspoon

**Canola oil,** 2 tablespoons

**Fresh ginger,** 1 tablespoon finely chopped

**Garlic,** 1 tablespoon finely chopped

**Baked tofu,** ½ lb (250 g), cut into ½-inch (12-mm) cubes

**Green onions,** 2, thinly sliced

**Roasted peanuts,** 2 tablespoons chopped

**Steamed rice,** for serving

**MAKES 4 SERVINGS**

Black bean–garlic sauce is a Chinese condiment made of fermented black beans, garlic, sugar, and red chiles. Just a little lends a lot of savory flavor to stir-fries, soups, and marinades. It keeps for months in the refrigerator once open. I like Lee Kum Kee brand.

1 Steam the eggplant in a steamer basket set over simmering water until tender, about 8 minutes. (Alternatively, working in batches, arrange the eggplant slices in a single layer on top of a double layer of paper towels and microwave on high until soft, 6—8 minutes.)

2 In a small bowl, whisk the black bean–garlic sauce, rice wine, soy sauce, Sriracha, vinegar, and sugar until the sugar dissolves.

3 In a large wok or deep-sided sauté pan, warm the oil over medium-high heat. Add the ginger and garlic and stir-fry until aromatic, 10 seconds. Add the eggplant and cook, stirring once or twice, until it begins to brown, 5 minutes. Reduce the heat to medium-low, add the tofu and the black bean–garlic sauce mixture, cover, and cook for 3 minutes, stirring once and lowering the heat if necessary to prevent scorching.

4 Divide the eggplant mixture among plates. Sprinkle with the green onions and peanuts and serve with the rice.

Here, grilled portobello mushrooms are loaded with a spicy chickpea mixture for a satisfying, protein-packed burger. The yogurt-based dressing adds even more protein and is reminiscent of creamy gyro sauce.

# Greek Portobello Burgers

**Extra-virgin olive oil,** 3 tablespoons

**Yellow onion,** ½ cup (2½ oz/75 g) finely chopped

**Red bell pepper,** ½ cup (6 oz/185 g) finely chopped

**Garlic,** 4 teaspoons finely chopped

**Ground cumin,** 1 teaspoon

**Chickpeas,** 1 can (15 oz/425 g), drained and rinsed

**Fresh bread crumbs,** 1 cup (2 oz/60 g)

**Fresh flat-leaf parsley,** 3 tablespoons finely chopped

**Lemon juice,** 2 tablespoons

**Lemon zest,** 1½ teaspoons finely grated

**Hot-pepper sauce,** 1 teaspoon

**Sea salt and freshly ground pepper**

**Portobello mushroom caps,** 4

**Red wine vinegar,** 1 tablespoon

**Ciabatta Rolls,** 4, split

**Plain yogurt,** ½ cup (4 oz/125 g)

**Cucumber,** ½ cup (2½ oz/75 g) seeded and finely chopped

**Shredded romaine lettuce,** 2 cups (2 oz/60 g)

**MAKES 4 SERVINGS**

1 Preheat a grill to medium heat. In a sauté pan over medium heat, warm 1 tablespoon of the oil. Add the onion and bell pepper and sauté until tender, 5 minutes. Add 2 teaspoons of the garlic and the cumin and sauté until aromatic, 30 seconds. Transfer the mixture to a large bowl and add the chickpeas, bread crumbs, parsley, lemon juice, zest, and hot sauce. Mash with a potato masher until most of the chickpeas have been smashed. Season to taste with salt and pepper and set aside.

2 Using a spoon, scrape out the black "gills" from the undersides of the mushrooms. In a small bowl, combine the remaining 2 tablespoons oil with the vinegar. Brush both sides of the mushrooms with the oil-vinegar mixture and season with salt and pepper. Grill the mushrooms, stemmed side down, covered, for 6 minutes. Remove from the grill. Divide the chickpea mixture among the mushroom caps, packing it down lightly. Return the mushrooms to the grill, filling side up. Cover and cook for 6 minutes more. For the last 3 minutes of grilling, place the rolls cut side down on the grill to warm.

3 In a bowl, combine the yogurt, cucumber, and remaining 2 teaspoons garlic and spread on the bottoms of the rolls. Divide the romaine among the roll bottoms and top with the mushrooms. Top with the roll tops.

The chickpea filling makes a great burger all by itself: Form the filling into 4 patties, then cook in a nonstick pan with a bit of olive oil. The chickpea patties freeze well, so if you are making this recipe, you can double the amount of filling and form half of it into patties. Wrap the patties tightly in plastic wrap, and store in the freezer for up to 3 months (thaw in the microwave before pan-frying).

This sandwich, popular street food in southern France, is basically a salade Niçoise on a bun: it features ripe tomatoes, shaved fennel, pickled beans, hardboiled eggs, and black olive aïoli stuffed in a crusty roll.

# Niçoise Salad Sandwiches

**Large egg yolk,** 1

**Lemon juice,** 1 teaspoon

**Garlic,** ½ teaspoon minced

**Extra-virgin olive oil,** ½ cup (4 fl oz/125 ml)

**Pitted Kalamata olives,** 1 tablespoon finely chopped

**Sea salt and freshly ground pepper**

**Large eggs,** 3

**Large baguette,** 1, halved horizontally

**Large heirloom tomato,** 1, cut into 8 slices

**Fennel bulb,** 1 cup (8 oz/250 g) very thinly sliced or shaved

**Pickled green beans,** ¾ cup (4 oz/140 g)

**Baby salad greens,** 1 cup (1 oz/30 g)

**MAKES 4 SANDWICHES**

1 In a mini food processor or bowl, combine the egg yolk with the lemon juice and garlic. Pour the olive oil into a spouted measuring cup or a clean squeeze bottle. Pulse or whisk in a few drops of oil, then slowly increase the speed to a slow, steady stream until all the oil has been added, pulsing or whisking constantly. Do not rush this or your aïoli will look scrambled and oily. Stir in the olives by hand, season to taste with salt and pepper, and set aside.

2 Bring a small saucepan of water to a boil. Gently lower the 4 eggs into the water, reduce the heat to medium, and simmer for 8½ minutes. Transfer the eggs to a bowl and cover with cold water. Once the eggs are cool to the touch, peel and slice them.

3 Spread the olive aïoli on the cut sides of the baguette. On the bottom half of the bread, layer the sliced egg, tomato, shaved fennel, green beans, and lettuce. Place the top of the bread on top of the sandwich, pressing lightly to close. Cut the completed sandwich into 4 sections.

Look for pickled green beans in the pickle section of grocery stores and farmers' markets. If you can't find pickled green beans, substitute pickled asparagus, beets, or your favorite pickled vegetable.

For softer, easier-to-eat sandwiches, divide the filling ingredients among 4 split ciabatta rolls.

Oven-crisped tortilla strips are layered with Mexican cheese and a quick and easy tomatillo-jalapeño sauce in this frugal pantry put-together. I like to top the dish with fried eggs for extra protein.

# Baked Tomatillo Chilaquiles

**Corn tortillas,** 6 inches (15 cm) in diameter, 12

**Extra-virgin olive oil,** 2 tablespoons plus 2 teaspoons

**Sea salt**

**Tomatillos,** 1 can (12 oz/375 g), drained

**Fresh cilantro,** ½ cup (¾ oz/20 g) chopped

**Vegetable broth,** ½ cup (4 fl oz/120 ml)

**Jalapeño chile,** 1, seeded and chopped

**Lime juice,** 1 tablespoon

**Garlic,** 1 teaspoon finely chopped

**Ground cumin,** 1 teaspoon

**Ground coriander,** 1 teaspoon

**Green onions,** 4, chopped, including tender green parts

**Asadero cheese or queso fresco,** 2 cups (5 oz/155 g) crumbled

**Large eggs,** 4

**Red chile flakes,** 1 pinch

**Ripe avocado,** 1, sliced

**Sour cream,** for garnish

**MAKES 4 SERVINGS**

For an even quicker dish, use purchased, thick-cut unsalted tortilla chips instead of baking the corn tortillas.

✕

For a more formal presentation, divide the ingredients among 4 (2-cup/16-fl oz/500-ml capacity) mini skillets and bake for 10 minutes. Be sure to set the hot pans on trivets and wrap a napkin around the handles to protect your hands.

1   Preheat the oven to 425°F (220°C). Line a rimmed baking sheet with parchment paper. Cut the tortillas into 1-by-2-inch (2.5-by-5-cm) strips. On the prepared sheet, toss the strips with the 2 tablespoons oil, then spread them out in a single layer. Sprinkle the strips with salt and bake until crisp, stirring once, 10—15 minutes.

2   Meanwhile, in a blender or food processor, combine the tomatillos, cilantro, broth, jalapeño, lime juice, garlic, cumin, coriander, ½ teaspoon salt, and half of the green onions. Purée until smooth.

3   Sprinkle half of the tortilla strips in an 8-inch (20-cm) square baking dish. Pour half of the reserved sauce over the top and sprinkle with half of the cheese. Top with the remaining tortilla strips, sauce, and cheese. Sprinkle with the remaining green onions. Bake until the cheese has melted and the sauce is bubbly, 15 minutes.

4   A few minutes before the chilaquiles are ready, cook the eggs: Warm the remaining 2 teaspoons oil in a large nonstick sauté pan over medium heat. Crack the eggs into the pan, sprinkle them with the chile flakes, and fry until the whites are set and the yolks are still runny, 4 minutes. Arrange the eggs on top of the chilaquiles, top with avocado and sour cream, and serve.

# Fall

# Fall

As the days get shorter, the leaves turn crimson, and a chill sets in, we all long for more substantial food, and nature delivers. There's a rainbow of firm-fleshed squashes to prepare with warm spices in stews, meaty mushrooms to tuck into pot pies and savory strudels, Brussels sprouts to roast and pair with buttery polenta, and soups, like golden corn and wild rice chowder, to soothe us. Curl up and get comfortable—this is a great time to cook.

## Smart Strategies for Fall Cooking

- To roast root vegetables without their sticking to the pan, preheat a heavy rimmed baking sheet in a 400°F (200°C) oven for at least 15 minutes. Toss roots cut in similar-sized pieces with plenty of olive oil, chopped fresh rosemary, salt, and pepper, then quickly place them into the hot pan. Roast until tender when pierced with a fork, 30—45 minutes.

- To safely cut up hard-shelled squashes, prick them with a fork or paring knife and zap for a few minutes in the microwave or bake them in a moderate oven for 15 minutes to soften them slightly. Plunge a sharp chef's knife into the squash near the stem and carefully push through the squash to the cutting board. If the knife sticks, don't try to pull it out; instead, tap on the knife with a rubber mallet to push the squash through. Repeat with the other side to cleave the vegetable in half.

- Try finishing dishes and making vinaigrettes with walnut, pumpkin seed, or hazelnut oil; they add a rich mouthfeel and buttery, roasted flavor to everyday dishes in fall.

## Super-Simple Fall Sides

- For a light spin on Waldorf salad, dice a variety of types of heirloom apples, then add toasted hazelnuts, sliced celery, and vanilla yogurt.

- For a quick gratin, blanch cauliflower or broccoli until just tender, toss with a mixture of mascarpone, a little Dijon mustard, and shredded Gruyère cheese and bake in a 350°F (180°C) oven until bubbly, 30 minutes.

- Chop a head of radicchio and soak it in ice water for 30 minutes to remove bitterness. Drain and toss with red wine vinegar, olive oil, and grainy mustard. Garnish with pomegranate seeds.

- Sizzle 2 sliced garlic cloves in 1 tablespoon of canola oil in a wok. Add chopped lacinato kale, a pinch of salt, and lots of pepper. Stir-fry over high heat until wilted and lightly charred. Off the heat, stir in a little soft goat cheese.

- Halve a dozen figs, sprinkle with Masala wine and a few pinches of brown sugar, and bake in a 400°F (200°C) oven until soft. Arrange on a bed of mixed greens with flecks of soft blue cheese.

Brussels sprouts become deliciously sweet when roasted and can be cooked in the time it takes to simmer the cheesy polenta in this recipe. Sweet-salty spiced walnuts add crunch to this southern-inspired dish.

# Brussels Sprouts with Cheddar Polenta and Spiced Walnuts

**FOR THE SPICED WALNUTS**

**Walnut pieces,** ¾ cup (3 oz/90 g), roughly chopped

**Unsalted butter,** 1 tablespoon, melted

**Brown sugar,** 2 teaspoons

**Fresh rosemary,** 1 teaspoon finely chopped

**Chili powder,** 1 teaspoon

**Garlic powder,** ¼ teaspoon

**Sea salt**

**Low-fat milk,** 1 cup (8 fl oz/250 ml)

**Dried bay leaf,** 1

**Brussels sprouts,** 1 lb (500 g), trimmed and halved lengthwise

**Extra-virgin olive oil,** 2 tablespoons

**Sea salt and freshly ground pepper**

**Yellow polenta,** 1 cup (5 oz/155 g)

**White Cheddar cheese,** 1 cup (4 oz/125 g) shredded

**MAKES 4 SERVINGS**

For a quick meal later in the week, double the polenta recipe, pour half of the batch into an 8-inch (20-cm) square baking pan, and refrigerate for up to 2 days. Slice the firmed polenta and pan-fry it in a few tablespoons of olive oil in a nonstick pan. Serve with warmed marinara sauce.

The spiced walnuts are so good, you may want to double them for future snacking.

1 To make the nuts, preheat the oven to 375°F (190°C). On a baking sheet, toss the walnuts with the melted butter, brown sugar, rosemary, chili powder, garlic powder, and ¾ teaspoon salt. Bake until the nuts are toasted, 8—10 minutes; set aside.

2 Increase the oven temperature to 400°F (200°C). In a saucepan, combine the milk and bay leaf with 4 cups (32 fl oz/1 l) water and bring to a boil over high heat. Meanwhile, toss the brussels sprouts with the oil on a rimmed baking sheet; season with salt and pepper. Arrange the brussels sprouts cut side down in a single layer and roast until just tender and browned on the bottom, 15—20 minutes.

4 Once the milk mixture is boiling, gradually whisk in the polenta. Reduce the heat to low and simmer, stirring frequently, until the polenta has thickened, about 18 minutes. Add the cheese and stir until melted. Season to taste with salt and pepper.

5 Divide the polenta among shallow bowls. Top with the brussels sprouts and spiced nuts, dividing evenly, and serve.

Kale leaves that have been massaged with oil and garlic and roasted until crisp make for a delicious healthy snack, but they are even better (and more satisfying) when loaded on top of this unconventional pizza.

# Crispy Kale, Mushroom, and Peppadew Pizza

**Cornmeal and all-purpose flour,** for dusting

**Lacinato, Russian, or curly kale,** 1 bunch (½ lb/250 g)

**Extra-virgin olive oil,** 3 tablespoons

**Garlic,** 2 teaspoons finely chopped

**Sea salt and freshly ground pepper**

**Maitake mushrooms,** 1½ cups (2½ oz/75 g), roughly chopped

**Pizza dough,** homemade (page 184) or purchased, 1 lb (500 g)

**Provolone cheese,** 10 thin slices (about 6 oz/185 g)

**Peppadew peppers,** ¼ cup (4 oz/ 125 g), thinly sliced

**MAKES 4 SERVINGS**

Maitake are wild mushrooms with a meaty texture and coral-like appearance. If you can't find them, swap in thinly sliced shiitake mushroom caps.

✕

Peppadew peppers are mildly spicy pickled peppers. Find them in the olive bar at some grocery stores or in glass jars.

1 Preheat the oven to 450°F (230°C). Sprinkle a pizza peel or large baking sheet with cornmeal.

2 Tear the kale leaves from the tough center stalks, discarding the stalks. Chop the leaves. In a large bowl, toss the chopped kale with 2 tablespoons of the oil, the garlic, and season to taste with salt and pepper. Set aside.

3 In a large sauté pan, warm the remaining 1 tablespoon oil over medium-high heat. Add the mushrooms and sauté until they are browned and slightly crisp, 4 minutes. Set aside.

4 On a lightly floured work surface, roll out the dough into a 16-inch (40-cm) oval. Place the pizza on the prepared peel. Arrange the cheese evenly over the pizza dough, leaving a ½-inch (12-mm) border uncovered. Spread the kale, mushrooms, and peppers evenly on top. Bake the pizza, rotating it once, until the crust is browned and the kale is beginning to crisp, 20 minutes. Cut the pizza into 8 squares and serve warm.

Instead of a side dish alongside roasted meats, as they usually do in Germany, I like to toss these little easy-to-make simmered dumplings with sautéed shredded brussels sprouts, chopped apple, and nutty aged cheese.

# Spaetzle with Cabbage, Apple, and Alpine Cheese

**Spaetzle Batter,** page 185

**Unsalted butter,** 3 tablespoons

**Extra-virgin olive oil,** 1 tablespoon

**Shallots,** ½ cup (2 oz/60 g) thinly sliced

**Garlic,** 2 teaspoons finely chopped

**Savoy or green cabbage,**
4 cups (12 oz/375 g) chopped

**Braeburn apple,** 1, peeled if desired, quartered, cored, and sliced

**Fresh thyme,** 2 teaspoons chopped

**Apple cider vinegar,** 2 tablespoons

**Aged cow's milk cheese,** such as Comté, Gruyère, or Raclette, 1 cup (4 oz/125 g) shredded

**Sea salt and freshly ground pepper**

**MAKES 4 SERVINGS**

1 Follow the instructions on page 185 to make the spaetzle batter. Bring a saucepan of salted water to a simmer over medium-low heat.

2 Hold the squeeze bottle in one hand over the water and squeeze out about a quarter of the batter in a slow, steady stream while snipping it into ¼-inch (6-mm) lengths with clean kitchen scissors as it comes out of the bottle. Stir and cook until the dumplings float to the surface, 1–2 minutes. Using a slotted spoon, lift the dumplings out of the water and transfer them to a large serving bowl with 2 tablespoons of the butter; cover and keep in a warm place. Repeat with the remaining batter.

3 In a large sauté pan, warm the oil and remaining 1 tablespoon butter over medium-high heat. Add the shallots and sauté until tender, 1½ minutes. Stir in the garlic and sauté for 20 seconds. Stir in the cabbage, apple, and thyme, and sauté until just tender and beginning to brown, 3 minutes. Add the vinegar and cook, scraping up the browned bits on the pan bottom, 30 seconds. Tip the contents of the pan into the dish with the spaetzle. Stir in the cheese and toss gently. Season to taste with salt and pepper and serve right away.

For a quicker preparation, substitute 1 lb (450 g) fresh gnocchi or ½ lb (225 g) wide egg noodles for the homemade spaetzle and prepare according to package instructions.

✖

Choose any herbs you like for this dish. I like a combination of flat-leaf parsley, thyme, rosemary, and chives.

✖

If you already own a spaetzle maker, by all means use it. Or try a colander with ¼-inch (6-mm) holes, food mill with the largest disk insert, or even a cleaned squeeze bottle for ketchup or mustard to make the dumplings.

This recipe is an ideal way to use leftover cooked rice. In fact, leftover rice is preferable to fresh, yielding perfect, separated grains when stir-fried. For a milder flavor, use broccolini instead of the Chinese broccoli.

# Fried Rice with Chinese Broccoli and Shiitakes

**Vegetable oil,** 2 tablespoons

**Garlic,** 1 tablespoon finely chopped

**Fresh ginger,** 2 teaspoons finely chopped

**Chinese broccoli (gai lan),** ½ lb (250 g), stems thinly sliced and florets roughly chopped

**Yellow onion,** ½, thinly sliced

**Shiitake mushrooms,** 1 cup (2 oz/60 g), stems discarded and caps sliced

**Cooked white or brown rice,** 4 cups (20 oz/625 g), broken up with your hands

**Soy sauce,** 3 tablespoons

**Chinese rice wine or sake,** 2 tablespoons

**Dark sesame oil,** ½ teaspoon

**Large egg,** 1

**Toasted salted cashews,** ½ cup (2½ oz/75 g)

**MAKES 4 SERVINGS**

1 In a wok or large, deep sauté pan, warm the oil over high heat. When the oil shimmers, add the garlic and ginger and stir-fry until aromatic, 10 seconds. Add the Chinese broccoli, onion, and mushrooms, and stir-fry until the onion is tender, 3 minutes.

2 Push the vegetables to the side of the wok and add the rice, letting it cook for 30 seconds without stirring. Stir in the soy sauce, wine, and sesame oil. Push the rice to the side of the wok and crack the egg into the wok. Cook, stirring constantly, until the egg is just set, 1 minute. Stir in the cashews and serve right away.

Soufflés have a reputation for being tricky to master, but not this recipe, which relies on a simple base of cottage cheese and whisked eggs. Serve with a radicchio salad to counter the richness.

# Cauliflower and Aged Gouda Soufflés

**Cauliflower florets,** ½ lb (250 g)

**Cottage cheese,** 1 cup (8 oz/250 g)

**Large eggs,** 4

**Freshly grated nutmeg,** ¼ teaspoon

**Cayenne pepper,** 1 pinch

**Sea salt and freshly ground black pepper**

**All-purpose flour,** ¼ cup (1½ oz/45 g)

**Aged Gouda cheese,** 1 cup (2½ oz/75 g) shredded

**MAKES 4 SERVINGS**

1 Preheat the oven to 350°F (180°C). Spray four 1-cup (8–fl oz/250-ml) ramekins with cooking spray and place them on a rimmed baking sheet.

2 In a steamer basket set over simmering water on the stove top, steam the cauliflower until just tender, 10 minutes. (Alternatively, place the cauliflower in a microwave-safe bowl with ¼ cup (2 fl oz/60 ml) water. Cover and microwave on high until tender, 3½ minutes.) Drain the cauliflower and chop it into ¼-inch (6-mm) pieces.

3 In a large bowl, whisk together the cottage cheese, eggs, nutmeg, and cayenne with ¼ teaspoon each salt and pepper. Gently fold in the chopped cauliflower. Sprinkle the flour on top and, using a rubber spatula, fold it in. Stir in half of the cheese. Divide the mixture among the prepared ramekins and sprinkle the remaining cheese on top. Bake until puffed and golden brown, 35—40 minutes. Serve warm.

Aged Gouda has a deep, nutty flavor and color. Look for it where artisan cheeses are sold (I like Rembrandt brand). Regular Gouda will work, too, but the flavor will be much milder.

✄

This recipe is also delicious when you substitute broccoli for the cauliflower and aged Cheddar for the Gouda.

V This rich Thai-style curry is usually made with beef and potatoes, but a hearty mixture of vegetables makes a fine stew without the meat. Massaman curry pastes vary in spiciness; adjust the amount according to taste.

# Massaman Curry with Kabocha Squash and Broccoli

**Kabocha squash,** 1 small (3 lb/1.5 kg)

**Canola oil,** 1 tablespoon

**Massaman curry paste,** 1½–2 tablespoons

**Yellow onion,** ½, thinly sliced

**Coconut milk,** 1 can (13.5 oz/415 ml)

**Broccoli florets,** 2 cups (6 oz/170 g) (2-inch/5-cm florets)

**Brown sugar,** 1 tablespoon firmly packed

**Tamarind concentrate,** 1½ teaspoons (optional)

**Roasted peanuts,** ½ cup (3 oz/90 g), roughly chopped

**Steamed jasmine rice,** for serving

**MAKES 4 SERVINGS**

1 Preheat the oven to 350°F (180°C). Put the whole squash on the oven rack and bake until slightly softened, about 10 minutes. (Alternatively, cook the squash in the microwave on high for 3 minutes.)

2 Using a chef's knife, halve the squash lengthwise. Scoop out the seeds and use a peeler or sharp paring knife to remove the skin. Cut the squash into 1-inch (2.5-cm) cubes. You will need 3 cups (24 oz/750 g) of squash cubes for this curry; freeze any remaining squash for another day (see Note).

3 In a saucepan, warm the oil over medium heat. Add the curry paste and cook, stirring constantly, until aromatic, 45 seconds. Add the onion and sauté until just softened, 1 minute. Add the squash, coconut milk, broccoli, brown sugar, and tamarind, if using, and bring to a simmer. Reduce the heat to low, cover, and cook, stirring occasionally, until the squash is tender, about 10 minutes.

4 Divide the curry among shallow bowls. Garnish with the peanuts and serve with the rice.

�֌

If your raw squash yields more than 3 cups (15 oz/470 g), turn the leftovers into an autumnal curried squash soup—sauté onion, garlic, ginger, and one or two carrots until tender. Add 4 cups (20 oz/625 g) squash cubes, 1 peeled and chopped tart apple, 4 cups (32 fl oz/1 l) vegetable broth, and a few teaspoons of curry powder. Simmer, covered, until tender, about 25 minutes. Purée the soup in a blender and season with salt and pepper.

✖

This updated version of the Indian classic saag paneer includes a healthy dose of sautéed leafy greens. Serve it with steamed basmati rice, whole wheat naan bread, and a dollop of sweet mango chutney or yogurt.

# Indian-Style Spiced Greens with Paneer

**Mustard greens,** 1 bunch

**Swiss chard,** 1 bunch

**Sugar,** 1 teaspoon

**Baby spinach,** 5 oz (155 g)

**Unsalted butter,** 2 tablespoons

**Yellow onion,** 1, finely chopped

**Cumin seeds,** 1 teaspoon

**Fresh ginger,** 1 tablespoon finely grated

**Garlic,** 2 teaspoons finely chopped

**Serrano chile,** 1, chopped

**Heavy cream,** ½ cup (4 fl oz/125 ml)

**Garam masala,** 1 teaspoon

**Paneer cheese,** ½ lb (225 g), cut into 1-inch (2.5-cm) cubes

**Sea salt and freshly ground pepper**

**MAKES 4 SERVINGS**

1 Tear the mustard green and chard leaves from the tough center stalks, discarding the stalks.

2 Bring a large pot of water to a boil. Add the sugar (this helps retain the bright color of the greens). Add the mustard greens to the boiling water and cook until wilted, 3 minutes. Using a slotted spoon, remove and drain the mustard green leaves, pressing on the greens to extract all the liquid. Cook and drain the chard in the same manner, cooking it for 2 minutes; cook and drain the spinach, cooking it as you did the mustard greens, for 1 minute. Transfer the wilted and drained greens to a cutting board or food processor and chop or pulse until finely chopped, set aside.

4 In a large sauté pan, melt the butter over medium heat. Add the onion and cumin and sauté until the onion is translucent and beginning to brown, 8 minutes. Add the ginger, garlic, and chile, and sauté until aromatic, 45 seconds. Stir in the greens, cream, and garam masala and bring to a simmer. Cook, stirring frequently, until the flavors have melded, 10 minutes.

5 Gently fold the paneer into the greens and simmer until heated through, 5 minutes. Season to taste with salt and pepper and serve right away.

To save time, purchase bags of prewashed and chopped winter greens (usually a mixture of kale, chard, collards, and mustard greens) at the supermarket. You will need about 12 ounces (375 g) of prechopped greens plus the baby spinach.

Frozen puff pastry is a boon to busy cooks, as it makes a great starter for all kinds of tarts. Here, it forms a flaky base for an elegant pear, blue cheese, and caramelized onion tart served with a crisp spinach salad alongside.

# Pear, Blue Cheese, and Onion Tart with Spinach Salad

Extra-virgin olive oil, 2½ tablespoons

Yellow onions, 2¼ cups (8 oz/250 g) thinly sliced

Dry white wine, ½ cup (4 fl oz/125 ml)

Fresh thyme, 2 teaspoons chopped

Sea salt and freshly ground pepper

All-purpose flour, for dusting

All-butter puff pastry, 1 sheet (9 oz/280 g)

Pears, 1½, cored and cut into ⅛-inch (3-mm) slices

Creamy blue cheese (such as Cashel), ¾ cup (3½ oz/105 g) crumbled

Baby spinach, 5 oz (155 g)

Lemon juice, 2 teaspoons

Large egg, 1, hard-boiled (see Note) and peeled

**MAKES 4 SERVINGS**

1 Preheat the oven to 400°F (200°C). Line a large rimmed baking sheet with parchment paper.

2 In a large sauté pan, warm 1 tablespoon of the oil over medium heat. Add the onions and cook, stirring frequently, until lightly browned, 8 minutes. Add the wine and simmer, scraping up the browned bits on the bottom of the pan, until the onions are very soft and evenly browned, 5 minutes. Stir in the thyme. Season with salt and pepper and set aside.

3 On a lightly floured surface, roll out the pastry to a 10-by-14-inch (25-by-35-cm) rectangle; transfer it to the prepared baking sheet. Prick the pastry all over with a fork and brush the edges with water. Fold up ½ inch (12 mm) of the dough around the perimeter and gently press down to create a thick border. Working inside the border, spread the onion mixture over the pastry. Lay the pear slices on top in a single layer. Sprinkle the cheese over the pears. Bake until the pastry is golden-brown and puffed, 25 minutes.

4 In a large bowl, toss the spinach with the lemon juice and the remaining 1½ tablespoons oil; season with salt and pepper. Push the egg through a small sieve over the salad. Cut the tart into 4 squares and serve with the salad alongside.

To hard-boil an egg, bring a small saucepan of water to a boil. Gently lower the egg into the water and set a timer for 9 minutes. Once the water begins to boil again, reduce the heat to maintain a gentle simmer until the timer goes off. (Do not cook the eggs longer than 10 minutes or the yolk will be dry and tinged with grey.) Transfer the eggs to a bowl of cold water to cool. Dry with paper towels and store in the refrigerator for up to 1 week.

Just a taste of this easy-to-prepare enchilada sauce, and you'll never go back to the canned version. The filling, a mix of corn, beans, and jack cheese, is so satisfying, even devoted carnivores won't miss the meat.

# Bean and Corn Enchiladas with Red Chile Sauce

**Enchilada Sauce,** page 186

**Corn tortillas** (8 inches/20 cm in diameter), 12

**Kidney beans,** 1 can (15½ oz/440 g), drained and rinsed

**Black beans,** 1 can (15 oz/425 g), drained and rinsed

**Frozen corn kernels,** 1 cup (6 oz/185 g), thawed

**Fresh cilantro,** ½ cup (⅔ oz/20 g) finely chopped

**Cheddar or jack cheese,** 1½ cups (6 oz/185 g) shredded

**Hulled pumpkin seeds (pepitas),** ½ cup (2½ oz/75 g)

**MAKES 4—6 SERVINGS**

1 Preheat the oven to 375°F (190°C). Spray a 9-by-13-inch (23-by-30-cm) baking dish with cooking spray

2 Follow the instructions on page 186 to make the enchilada sauce. Spoon ½ cup (4 fl oz/125 ml) of the sauce into the bottom of the baking dish.

3 Wrap the tortillas in damp paper towels, then wrap them in a layer of foil, and bake them for 10 minutes. (Alternatively, wrap them in damp paper towels and microwave on high until pliable, 30 seconds.)

4 In a bowl, combine the kidney beans, black beans, corn, cilantro, and 1 cup (4 oz/125 g) of the cheese. Using a potato masher, mash the mixture until about half of the beans are mashed. Place ¼ cup (4 oz/115 g) of the bean filling on the lower third of each tortilla, roll up tightly, and arrange seam side down in the baking dish. Cover with the remaining enchilada sauce, cheese, and pepitas, and bake until the sauce is bubbly and the cheese is melted, 25 minutes.

5 Let the enchiladas stand for a few minutes in the pan to cool slightly, then serve with a wide spatula.

Don't mistake chili powder—the blend of spices and salt used for the stew of the same name—with zesty New Mexican chile powder, which is made from purely ground chiles. Look for it at gourmet shops and grocery stores that carry Latino foods.

(V) Based on the traditional Indian pilaf, this quick rice supper stars sweet roasted squash, bell peppers, and carrots. Serve with sliced cucumbers dressed with plain yogurt, lime juice, and a pinch of ground cumin.

# Roasted Vegetable Biryani

**Butternut squash,** 1 small (1½ lb/ 750 g), peeled and cut into 1-inch (2.5-cm) cubes

**Carrots,** 2 large, quartered lengthwise and cut into 2-inch (5-cm) segments

**Red bell pepper,** 1 small, cut into 1-inch (2.5-cm) strips

**Extra-virgin olive oil,** 4 tablespoons

**Curry powder,** 2 teaspoons

**Sea salt and freshly ground pepper**

**Yellow onion,** 2 cups (7 oz/220 g) thinly sliced

**Jalapeño chile,** 1, chopped

**Cinnamon stick,** 1, broken in half

**Whole cloves,** 4

**Green cardamom pods,** 6

**Cumin seeds,** 1 teaspoon

**Garlic,** 4 cloves, thinly sliced

**Fresh ginger,** 1 tablespoon finely chopped

**Basmati rice,** 1 cup (7 oz/220 g)

**Vegetable broth,** 2 cups (16 fl oz/ 500 ml)

**Golden raisins or currants,** 2 tablespoons

**Turmeric,** ½ teaspoon

**Roasted cashews,** ½ cup (2⅔ oz/75 g)

**MAKES 4 SERVINGS**

Resist the urge to stir the rice while it cooks, which will only break up the rice grains and make it mushy.

1 Preheat the oven to 425°F (220°C). On a rimmed baking sheet, toss the squash, carrots, and bell pepper with 2 tablespoons of the oil, the curry powder, and a few pinches of salt. Roast the vegetables, stirring once, until tender when pierced with a fork, 20—25 minutes.

2 Meanwhile, in a large sauté pan, warm the remaining 2 tablespoons oil over medium heat. Add the onion, jalapeño, cinnamon, cloves, cardamom, and cumin, and cook, stirring frequently, until the onions begin to brown, 6 minutes. Add the garlic and ginger and cook until aromatic, 1 minute. Stir in the rice and cook for 1 minute. Add the broth, raisins, and turmeric, and bring to a simmer. Reduce the heat to low, cover, and simmer gently until the liquid has been absorbed and the rice is tender, 10—12 minutes. Remove from heat and keep covered until the vegetables have finished roasting.

3 Gently fold the roasted vegetables and cashews into the rice. Season to taste with salt and pepper and serve. Set the spices aside as diners eat.

In this cozy recipe, I fry sage leaves in olive oil until crisp, then I braise cubes of winter squash with the infused oil to make a chunky sauce for the pasta. Serve with a roasted beet, walnut, and blue cheese salad.

# Penne with Winter Squash and Fried Sage

**Extra-virgin olive oil,** 3 tablespoons

**Fresh sage leaves,** ⅓ cup (⅓ oz/10 g) packed (about 25 large leaves)

**Butternut, hubbard, or acorn squash,** 2¼ lb (about 1 kg), peeled, seeded and cut into ¾-inch (2-cm) cubes

**Sea salt and freshly ground black pepper**

**Garlic,** 2 tablespoons finely chopped

**Vegetable broth,** 1 cup (8 fl oz/ 250 ml)

**Red pepper flakes,** 1 pinch

**Penne pasta,** ¾ lb (375 g)

**Parmesan cheese,** ⅓ cup (1⅓ oz/40 g) grated

**Lemon juice,** 4 teaspoons

**MAKES 4 SERVINGS**

Not keen on prepping winter squash? Buy pre-diced and peeled butternut squash from the produce department of the grocery store. You may need to cut the chunks into smaller, bite-size pieces. Just don't be tempted to use frozen squash here: It'll turn to mush instantly.

1 Bring a large pot of salted water to boil. Meanwhile, in a large sauté pan, warm the oil over medium-high heat. Working in batches, fry the sage leaves until crisp and beginning to brown, 3 minutes. Using tongs, transfer the leaves to a paper towel-lined plate.

2 Add the squash to the pan with the sage oil and season with salt and pepper. Cook, stirring once, until the squash begins to caramelize, 4 minutes. Reduce the heat to medium, push the squash aside a bit, and add the garlic; sauté the garlic until fragrant, 20 seconds. Add the broth and red pepper flakes, cover, and simmer until the squash is tender when pierced with a fork, about 3 minutes.

3 Add the pasta to the boiling water and cook until al dente according to package instructions. Reserve ½ cup (4 fl oz/125 ml) of the cooking water and drain the pasta. Transfer the pasta to the pan with the squash along with the cheese and lemon juice. Stir gently to combine, adding the reserved pasta cooking water 1 tablespoon at a time if needed to moisten the mixture. Season to taste with salt and pepper. Crumble the fried sage leaves over the top and serve.

This savory strudel features sautéed mushrooms, sweet chestnuts, and nutty Gruyère cheese rolled into a crisp pastry shell. Though quick to make, it is elegant enough to serve as a vegetarian main course for a holiday feast.

# Mushroom-Chestnut Strudel

**Olive oil,** 1 tablespoon

**Leeks,** 2 (each about 6 oz/185 g), white and light-green parts only, thinly sliced

**Mixed wild mushrooms,** ½ lb (250 g), sliced

**Cremini mushrooms,** ½ lb (250 g), sliced

**Fresh thyme,** 1 tablespoon, chopped

**Garlic,** 2 teaspoons minced

**Sea salt and freshly ground pepper**

**Marsala wine,** ¼ cup (2 fl oz/60 ml)

**Cooked, peeled chestnuts,** ¼ lb (125 g), roughly chopped

**Filo dough,** 12 sheets, thawed

**Unsalted butter,** ⅓ cup (3 oz/90 g), melted

**Fresh whole-wheat or rye bread crumbs,** ½ cup (1 oz/30 g)

**Gruyère cheese,** 1¼ cups (5 oz/155 g) shredded

**MAKES 4 SERVINGS**

Choose your favorite mixture of wild mushrooms for this recipe, such as porcini, chanterelle, morel, and maitake.

✄

To cut down on prep work, look for pre-sliced cremini mushrooms in the produce department.

✄

Roasted, peeled chestnuts are available vacuum-packed or in jars at well-stocked supermarkets.

1 Preheat the oven to 400°F (200°C). Line a large rimmed baking sheet with parchment paper. In a 14-inch (35-cm) frying pan, warm the oil over medium-high heat. Add the leeks and sauté until tender, 3 minutes. Add all of the mushrooms, the thyme, garlic, and a sprinkle of salt. Sauté until the mushrooms release their liquid and begin to brown, 8 minutes. Add the Marsala and simmer, scraping up the browned bits from the pan bottom, until the liquid evaporates. Add the chestnuts and season with salt and pepper. Scrape the mixture into a bowl; refrigerate until needed.

2 Place 1 piece of filo dough on a large cutting board with the long side facing you. Brush with some of the melted butter and sprinkle evenly with some of the bread crumbs. Top with another sheet of filo, brush with butter, and sprinkle with crumbs. Repeat, buttering and sprinkling the remaining filo sheets; do not add crumbs to the final sheet.

3 Transfer the stacked filo to the baking sheet. Leaving a 1-inch (2.5-cm) border on the side closest to you, spread the mushroom mixture lengthwise in a strip on the dough. Sprinkle with the cheese. Lift the filo up and over the filling and then roll up into a tight cylinder with the seam side down. Brush the outside of the strudel with butter. Bake until golden brown, 25 minutes.

4 Let the strudel cool for 5 minutes. With a sharp serrated knife, slice the strudel into eight slices and serve.

This Mexican sandwich is usually stuffed with meats, but vegetarian fillings—mashed black beans, creamy avocados, fresh vegetables, gooey melted cheese, and pickled jalapeños—make this version a standout.

# Grilled Cheese Torta with Black Beans and Avocado

**Extra-virgin olive oil,** 1 tablespoon

**Garlic,** 1 tablespoon finely chopped

**Black beans,** 1 can (15 oz/425 g), drained and rinsed

**Ground cumin,** 1 teaspoon

**Hot-pepper sauce,** 2 teaspoons

**Sea salt**

**Square sandwich rolls,** 4 (I like La Brea Bakery's ciabatta rolls)

**Provolone cheese,** 4 slices

**Tomato,** 1, cored and thinly sliced

**Avocado,** 1 large ripe, pitted and sliced

**Small red onion,** ½, thinly sliced

**Pickled jalapeño chiles,** ¼ cup (2 oz/60 g) sliced

**Canola oil,** 2 teaspoons (optional)

**MAKES 4 SERVINGS**

For a milder sandwich, use jarred roasted poblano chiles or red bell peppers instead of the jalapeño chiles.

1　If you're using a sandwich grill or press, turn it on to preheat. In a small saucepan, warm the oil over medium heat. Add the garlic and sauté until aromatic, 30 seconds. Add the beans and, using a potato masher, mash them until they are mostly smooth. Add the cumin, hot sauce, and ½ cup (4 fl oz/ 125 ml) water. Bring to a simmer, stirring occasionally, until the beans are thickened, 10 minutes. Season to taste with salt.

2　Using a serrated knife, slice open the rolls horizontally, leaving them partially attached on one side. Spread the bottom half of the rolls with the beans, dividing evenly. Top with the cheese, tomato, avocado, onion, and jalapeño, dividing the ingredients evenly among the rolls.

3　Grill the sandwiches in a sandwich press until the cheese has melted, 5 minutes. (If you don't have a sandwich press, warm the canola oil in a large frying pan over medium heat. Place the sandwiches in the pan and place a sandwich weight or heavy pan on top of the sandwiches to weigh them down a bit. Grill until the cheese has melted, 5 minutes.) Cut the sandwiches in half and serve.

(V) Following the Mediterranean tradition of mezze, this easy supper consists of two salads: a smoky grilled eggplant salad and a cooling tomato salad—plus marinated olives and grilled spiced flatbread.

# Mediterranean Mezze Plate

**Mixed olives,** 1 cup (5 oz/155 g)

**Extra-virgin olive oil,** ½ cup (4 fl oz/125 ml) plus 2 teaspoons

**Garlic,** 2 large cloves, thinly sliced

**Fennel seeds,** 1 teaspoon

**Cumin seeds,** ½ teaspoon

**Heirloom tomatoes,** ½ lb (250 g)

**Sea salt and freshly ground pepper**

**Chickpeas,** 1 can (14 oz/440 g), drained and rinsed

**Green onions,** ¼ cup (¾ oz/20 g) sliced

**Fresh basil leaves,** ½ cup (½ oz/15 g), torn

**Red wine vinegar,** 1 tablespoon

**Sweet smoked paprika,** ½ teaspoon

**Eggplant,** 2 (2 lb/1kg total), sliced lengthwise into 1-inch (2.5-cm) slices

**Anaheim chile,** 1

**Purchased flatbread,** 9 oz (280 g)

**Za'atar,** 2 teaspoons

**Lemon juice,** 2 tablespoons

**Ground cumin,** 1 teaspoon

**MAKES 4 SERVINGS**

Za'atar is an herb-and-sesame blend that lends an earthy flavor to grilled vegetables, bread, and tomato salads. Find it at Middle Eastern markets and online.

✄

Choose a selection of Mediterranean-style olives that you like, such as Castelvetrano, Niçoise, and Kalamata. Set out a small dish for the pits.

✄

If you want to skip the salting step, substitute quartered cherry tomatoes for the heirlooms in the tomato salad (pictured).

1 Preheat a grill to medium-high heat. In a small grillproof saucepan, combine the olives, ¼ cup (2 fl oz/60 ml) oil, the garlic, fennel seeds, and cumin seeds. Cover with foil and place on the coolest part of the grill.

2 Chop the tomatoes into bite-size pieces, place them in a colander, and sprinkle with salt. Let them drain for 10 minutes; pat dry with paper towels. Transfer to a bowl and add the chickpeas, green onions, basil, vinegar, and 1 tablespoon of the oil. Season to taste with salt and pepper and set aside.

3 Mix 3 tablespoons of the oil with the smoked paprika and brush the mixture on both sides of the eggplant. Grill the eggplant and chile, turning, until the vegetables are tender, 5—6 minutes per side. Brush the flatbread with the remaining 2 teaspoons oil and grill until warm, 2 minutes per side. Sprinkle the bread with the za'atar, wrap it in foil, and keep in a warm place.

4 Scrape the blackened skins and seeds from the chile and discard. Roughly chop the chile and eggplant and place them in a serving bowl. Add the lemon juice and ground cumin, mix well, and season to taste with salt and pepper.

5 Serve the eggplant salad, tomato salad, and warm olives with the warm flatbread alongside.

Posole is traditionally made with long-simmered pork and dried hominy. This meatless version is equally delicious and comes together in a fraction of the time, thanks to the use of canned hominy.

# Red Hominy Stew

**Extra-virgin olive oil,** 1 tablespoon

**Yellow onion,** 1½ cups (7½ oz/215 g) finely chopped

**Carrot,** 1, peeled and thinly sliced

**Garlic,** 1 tablespoon finely chopped

**Canned chipotle chiles in adobo,** 1 tablespoon chopped

**Ground cumin,** 1½ teaspoons

**Dried Mexican oregano,** 1½ teaspoons

**Ancho chile powder,** 1 teaspoon

**White hominy,** 1 large can (29 oz/910 g), drained

**Vegetable broth,** 2 cups (16 fl oz/ 500 ml)

**Canned, diced fire-roasted tomatoes in juice,** ½ cup (3 oz/90 g)

**Yukon Gold potato,** 1, peeled and cut into ½-inch (12-mm) cubes

**Lime juice,** 1 tablespoon

**Finely grated lime zest,** 1½ teaspoons

**Sea salt and freshly ground pepper**

**Avocado,** 1 large, pitted and diced

**Radishes,** 8, thinly sliced

**Fresh cilantro,** ½ cup (⅔ oz/20 g) chopped

**Cotija cheese,** ½ cup (2½ oz/75 g) crumbled

**Warm corn tortillas or tortilla chips,** for serving

**MAKES 4 SERVINGS**

Since a little goes a long way with potent chipotle chiles, it can take a long time to use up a whole can. Freeze any remaining chiles and sauce in a sealable plastic bag in the freezer and use a serrated knife to chop off only what you need for a recipe. The chiles will last in the freezer for up to 3 months before their flavor begins to fade.

1  In a Dutch oven or other large, heavy pot, warm the oil over medium-high heat. Add the onion and carrot and cook until just tender, 4 minutes. Add the garlic and cook until fragrant, 30 seconds. Add the chipotle chiles, cumin, oregano, and chile powder, and sauté for about 10 seconds.

2  Stir in the hominy, broth, tomatoes, potato, and 2 cups (16 fl oz/500 ml) water. Bring to a simmer, cover, and reduce heat to low. Simmer gently, stirring occasionally, until the potato is tender, 20 minutes. Add the lime juice and zest and season to taste with salt and pepper.

3  Set out a platter or individual bowls of the avocado, radishes, cilantro, and cheese. Divide the stew among soup bowls, inviting diners to garnish their own portions to their liking. Pass the tortillas at the table.

Rich fontina cheese, slightly bitter radicchio, and crunchy roasted hazelnuts accent this easy pasta dish. Serve with glasses of Nebbiolo and you've got a cozy dinner in minutes flat. Don't forget the garlic bread!

# Rotini with Radicchio, Fontina, and Hazelnuts

**Unsalted butter,** 2 tablespoons

**Garlic,** 3 large cloves, thinly sliced

**Fresh rosemary,** 1 tablespoon finely chopped

**Radicchio,** 1 head, cored and chopped

**Rotini pasta,** ¾ lb (375 g)

**Fontina cheese,** ⅓ lb (155 g), cut into ¼-inch (6-mm) cubes

**Sea salt and freshly ground pepper**

**Roasted chopped hazelnuts,** ½ cup (2½ oz/75 g)

**MAKES 4 SERVINGS**

1 Bring a large pot of salted water to a boil. Meanwhile, melt the butter in a large sauté pan over medium heat. Add the garlic and rosemary and cook, stirring constantly, 1 minute. Add the radicchio and cook, stirring frequently, until it has wilted and is beginning to brown, 4 minutes. Remove from the heat.

2 Add the pasta to the boiling water and cook until al dente according to the package directions. Reserve ½ cup (4 fl oz/125 ml) of the pasta cooking water and drain the pasta.

3 Return the sauté pan to medium heat and stir in the pasta, cheese, and reserved pasta cooking water. Cook and toss until the cheese is melted. Season to taste with salt and pepper and divide among 4 bowls. Sprinkle the hazelnuts on top and serve right away.

✕

Not all fontina cheese is crafted the same way or posses the same nutty-meets-funky aroma and buttery flavor. I prefer Fontina Val D'Aosta, which is made in Northwest Italy and can be found wherever fine cheeses are sold.

✕

This easy, creamy chowder doubles the sweet corn flavor by using fresh kernels shaved from the cob, plus the cobs themselves to flavor the broth. The wild rice is cooked separately to preserve its texture.

# Wild Rice Corn Chowder

**Quick-cooking wild rice,** ⅓ cup (2 oz/60 g), rinsed

**Sea salt and freshly ground pepper**

**Unsalted butter,** 3 tablespoons

**Yellow onion,** 1 cup (5 oz/155 g) finely chopped

**Celery,** 1 stalk, chopped

**Carrot,** 1, peeled and finely chopped

**Garlic,** 1 teaspoon finely chopped

**Dried thyme,** 1 teaspoon

**All-purpose flour,** ¼ cup (1½ oz/45 g)

**Vegetable broth,** 4 cups (32 fl oz/1 l)

**Dry sherry or dry white wine,** ¼ cup (2 fl oz/60 ml)

**Fresh corn,** 4 ears, shucked, kernels cut from the cobs, cobs reserved

**Yukon Gold potato,** 1, peeled and cut into ½-inch (12-mm) cubes

**Sweet smoked paprika,** ½ teaspoon

**Heavy cream,** 2 tablespoons

**Fresh lemon juice,** 1 tablespoon

**MAKES 4 SERVINGS**

1 In a small saucepan, combine the wild rice, 1½ cups (12 fl oz/240 ml) water, and ¼ teaspoon salt. Bring the water to a boil over high heat, then reduce the heat to medium-low, cover, and simmer until the rice is tender, 35—40 minutes.

2 Meanwhile, in another saucepan, melt the butter over medium heat. Add the onion, celery, carrot, garlic, and thyme, and sauté until the onion is translucent, 4 minutes. Add the flour and cook, stirring, 1 minute. Stir in the broth and sherry until combined.

3 Add the corn kernels, corncobs, potato, and paprika to the pan, and bring to a simmer over medium heat. Cover, reduce the heat to low, and cook, stirring occasionally, until the potatoes are tender, about 20 minutes. Remove the cobs from the soup and discard.

4 When the rice is tender, drain it and add it to the soup along with the cream and cook until heated through, 5 minutes. Add the lemon juice to taste, season with salt and pepper, and serve.

"Quick-cooking" wild rice has kernels that have been scratched, so water can penetrate them more quickly. This reduces the cooking time from 50 to about 35 minutes. Because wild rice is a healthy whole grain (and a great addition to salad and soups), I often cook a large batch and keep a stash in sealable plastic bags in the freezer for impromptu meals.

There are endless options of fillings and toppings for these Japanese-style pancakes. I use a traditional trio of cabbage, carrot, and bean sprouts here, but you can also get creative: try corn, snow peas, or shredded kale.

# Savory Japanese Vegetable Pancakes

Ketchup, ⅓ cup (3 fl oz/80 ml)

Vegetarian Worcestershire sauce, 2 tablespoons

Soy sauce, 2 teaspoons

Brown sugar, 2 teaspoons

All-purpose flour, 2 cups (10 oz/315 g)

Baking powder, 2 teaspoons

Sugar, 2 teaspoons

Sea salt and freshly ground pepper

Vegetable broth or vegetarian dashi, 2 cups (16 fl oz/500 ml)

Large eggs, 4

Small head green cabbage, ½, shredded (about 5 cups/15 oz/470 g)

Carrot, 1 cup (5 oz/140 g) shredded

Bean sprouts, 1 cup (1 oz/30 g)

Green onions, 2, thinly sliced

Canola oil, 2 tablespoons

Mayonnaise, ¼ cup (2 fl oz/60 ml)

**MAKES 4 SERVINGS**

1 Preheat the oven to 200°F (95°C). To make the sauce, in a bowl, combine the ketchup, Worcestershire, soy sauce, and brown sugar. Stir well and set aside.

2 To make the pancakes, in a large bowl, whisk together the flour, baking powder, and sugar with 1 teaspoon each salt and pepper. In a small bowl, whisk together the broth and eggs. Add the wet ingredients to the dry ingredients and whisk until smooth. Add the cabbage, carrot, bean sprouts, and green onions and stir to combine.

3 In a large nonstick frying pan, warm 1½ teaspoons of the oil over medium-low heat. Ladle one-fourth of the batter into the pan to form a pancake that is about 7 inches (18 cm) in diameter. Cook until the edges are set and the bottom of the pancake is lightly browned, 4 minutes. Using a spatula, flip the pancake and cook until set in the middle, about 2 minutes. Transfer the pancake to a baking sheet and keep it warm in the oven. Repeat with the remaining oil and batter to make 3 more pancakes.

4 In a small bowl, mix the mayonnaise with 2 tablespoons water. Drizzle the sauce and mayonnaise over the pancakes in a crosshatch pattern and serve right away.

✖

For a heartier, Japanese-style meal, serve this with a seaweed and cucumber salad dressed with rice vinegar or a bowl of hot soba noodles dressed with dark sesame oil and soy sauce.

✖

# Winter

# Winter

When it's cold and blustery outside, we tend to crave comforting and nourishing foods to sustain us. In this chapter you'll find quick, filling dishes like creamy mushroom paprikash, and warming soups like cheddar broccoli and apple–celery root. There are also a handful of recipes with bright flavors, like Jamaican bean cakes with habanero chile, and quinoa pasta with peppery broccoli rabe, so you can keep your palate out of hibernation all winter long.

## Smart Strategies For Winter Cooking

- Hearty winter greens like kale and collards have a tough stem that runs up the center of their leaves. To remove it efficiently, fold the leaf in half lengthwise and tear the stem or rib away from the tender leaves on either side.

- Winter is the best time for citrus fruit lovers. Try some of the exciting heirloom varieties like juicy Cara Cara oranges, sweet Satsuma tangerines, and tangy tangelos in salads and desserts.

- To ward off bugs when your immunity is low, include fermented foods like kimchi, sauerkraut, and miso in your winter menus to help keep your gut flora healthy.

- Incorporate tart and pungent ingredients like fresh ginger, hot chilies, tamarind, citrus zest, and blue cheese into dishes to keep meals interesting all season long.

- One of my favorite winter treats is vanilla ice cream with warm rum-raisin sauce. To make the sauce, melt 2 tablespoons butter over medium heat. Add ½ cup (3½ oz/105 g) brown sugar and cook until dissolved. Add 1 cup (6 oz/185 g) golden raisins, ¼ cup (2 fl oz/60 ml) apple cider, ¼ cup (2 fl oz/60 ml) dark rum, 1 cinnamon stick, and ½ teaspoon salt and simmer until syrupy.

## Super-Simple Winter Sides

- For a quick salad to serve with rich, creamy foods, cut the peel away from ruby red grapefruit and cut into ¼-inch (6-mm) thick slices. Shave fennel over the top and drizzle with honey.

- Sauté ½ sliced red onion in 2 tablespoons butter until soft. Add 6 cups (18 oz/560 g) shredded red cabbage, 1 teaspoon of caraway seeds, and 2 pinches of salt. Sauté until tender. Add red wine vinegar and freshly grated pepper to taste.

- Place 1 pound (500 g) of peeled russet potato chunks in a saucepan of cold salted water. Bring to a boil and cook until tender, 15—20 minutes. Drain and mash with 2 tablespoons each butter and milk. Season lightly with freshly grated nutmeg and salt.

- For a refreshing winter slaw, peel and grate a large celery root and toss with lemon juice, extra-virgin olive oil, capers, and chopped green apple.

Potatoes, when thinly sliced and sprinkled with rosemary and blue cheese, become a buttery treat on a whole-wheat pizza base. The kale pesto moistens the dough and gives the pizza a satisfying, earthy flavor.

# Potato and Blue Cheese Pizza with Kale Pesto

**Small Yukon gold potatoes,** 2

**Pizza Dough,** 1 lb (500 g), homemade (page 184) or purchased

**Kale Pesto,** page 186

**Blue cheese,** ½ cup (2½ oz/75 g) crumbled

**Mozzarella cheese,** 1 cup (4 oz/125 g) shredded

**Fresh rosemary,** 2 teaspoons finely chopped

**MAKES 4 SERVINGS**

1 Place a pizza stone in the lower third of the oven and preheat the oven to 450°F (230°C).

2 Cut the potatoes in half, then place the cut sides down on a cutting board and cut into ⅛-inch (3-mm) slices. (Alternatively, thinly slice the potatoes using a mandoline.)

3 Divide the dough in half and roll it out on a lightly floured surface into two 10- to 12-inch (25- to 30-cm) rounds. Place the rounds on separate pieces of parchment paper. Spread the kale pesto evenly on the dough rounds. Top with the potatoes, blue cheese, mozzarella, and rosemary, dividing evenly. Slide one of the pizzas (still on the parchment) onto the baking stone and bake until the crust is golden brown and the cheese is bubbly, 15 minutes.

4 Cut the pizza into wedges and serve. Bake the second pizza while enjoying the first one.

Instead of making homemade kale pesto, you can skip a step and use store-bought basil pesto here for equally delicious results.

This North African–inspired dish features cauliflower florets and sliced winter squash rubbed with harissa, a fiery chile-and-spice paste. The vegetables are served on fregola, toasted pasta spheres from Sardinia.

# Fregola with Cauliflower, Delicata Squash, and Harissa

**Delicata squash,** 2

**Cauliflower,** 1 head (about 1½ lb/ 750 g), cut into large florets

**Shallots,** 4, cut into ½-inch (12-mm) thick wedges, plus ¼ cup (1 oz/30 g) thinly sliced shallot

**Prepared harissa,** 1—2 tablespoons

**Extra-virgin olive oil,** 3 tablespoons

**Sea salt and freshly ground pepper**

**Garlic,** 1 tablespoon thinly sliced

**Fregola,** 1 cup (7 oz/200 g)

**Vegetable broth,** 2 cups (16 fl oz/ 500 ml)

**Saffron,** 1 pinch

**Plain Greek yogurt,** ½ cup (4 oz/125 g)

**Fresh cilantro,** 3 tablespoons chopped

**MAKES 4 SERVINGS**

Harissa is a North African chile-and-spice paste that comes in tubes. Look for harissa at gourmet grocery stores, specialty food shops, and online. Be sure to taste the harissa before adding it to recipes, as the condiment varies widely in spiciness from brand to brand.

✕

Instead of the fregola, you can also serve this dish over Israeli couscous or another small pasta shape such as orzo.

1 Preheat the oven to 400°F (200°C). Halve the squash lengthwise and scoop out the seeds. Cut the squash crosswise into ½-inch (12-mm) half moon–shaped slices.

2 In a large bowl, combine the squash, cauliflower, shallot wedges, harissa, and 2 tablespoons of the olive oil, stirring to coat. On a rimmed baking sheet, spread the vegetables in a single layer. Sprinkle with salt and pepper and bake until the squash and cauliflower are easily pierced with a fork, 30—40 minutes.

3 While the vegetables roast, make the fregola: In a saucepan, warm the remaining 1 tablespoon oil over medium heat. Add the sliced shallot and garlic and sauté until tender, 2 minutes. Stir in the fregola, add the broth and saffron, and bring to a simmer. Reduce the heat to maintain a gentle simmer, cover, and cook until the fregola is tender, 20—25 minutes. Season to taste with salt and pepper.

4 In a small serving bowl, whisk together the yogurt and cilantro. Transfer the fregola to a large, shallow serving bowl. Spoon the roasted vegetables in the center of the bowl and spoon the yogurt sauce over the top.

Sharp cheddar, microbrewed ale, and apple slices elevate this open-faced grilled sandwich to a chic dinner on the fly. A peppery watercress salad counters the richness of the cheese topping.

# Welsh Rarebit with Tangy Watercress Salad

If you're a strict vegetarian, be sure to check the label on the Worcestershire sauce, as some contain anchovies. Substitute leftover roasted cauliflower, fennel, or carrots for the apples.

✕

This recipe is easily adaptable for entertaining. To make a wintry first course for a party of 8, follow the recipe, but omit the romaine. Arrange the toasts on a platter or individual plates.

**Crusty country bread,** 1 loaf (1 lb/ 500 g), cut into 8 thick slices

**Apple,** 1, preferably Fuji, cored and thinly sliced

**Watercress,** 1 bunch (about 2¼ cups/ 2¼ oz), tough stems removed

**Romaine lettuce,** 1½ cups (1½ oz/ 45 g) chopped

**Extra-virgin olive oil,** 1 tablespoon

**Lemon juice,** 2 teaspoons

**Fleur de sel or flaky sea salt**

**Freshly ground pepper**

**Unsalted butter,** 3 tablespoons

**All-purpose flour,** 3 tablespoons

**Pale ale,** ½ cup (4 fl oz/125 ml)

**Worcestershire sauce,** 2 teaspoons

**Grainy mustard,** 1 teaspoon

**Aged Cheddar cheese,** ½ lb (250 g), shredded

**MAKES 4 SERVINGS**

1 Place a rack in the top third of the oven, about 4 inches (10 cm) below the broiling element, and preheat the broiler. On a rimmed baking sheet, arrange the bread slices in a single layer and broil until lightly browned, about 1 minute. Remove the baking sheet from the oven and leave the broiler on. Arrange the apple slices in even layers on top of the bread slices; set aside. In a large bowl, toss the watercress and romaine with the oil and lemon juice and season to taste with fleur de sel and pepper; set aside.

2 In a small saucepan, melt the butter over medium-low heat. Whisk in the flour and cook for 1 minute. Whisk in the beer, and cook until the mixture is thick and bubbly, 1 minute. Reduce the heat to low and add the Worcestershire sauce, mustard, and a handful of the cheese. Cook until the cheese has melted, whisking in only one direction to prevent the sauce from becoming stringy. Continue adding cheese by the handful and stirring it until melted before adding the next handful, until all of the cheese has been added and melted. The mixture will be very thick and pastelike.

3 Working quickly, spread the cheese mixture evenly over the apples. Broil until the cheese is bubbly and browned in places, about 1 minute. Place 2 cheese toasts on each plate, top with a big mound of salad, and serve.

(V) This silky soup tastes creamy but is actually dairy-free: The starch in the root vegetables thickens the soup and imparts its dreamy texture. Serve with warm whole-grain bread to mop up every last drop of soup.

# Celery Root Soup with Truffle Oil

**Extra-virgin olive oil,** 1 tablespoon

**Yellow onion,** 1½ cups (7½ oz/235 g) finely chopped

**Parsnip,** 1, peeled and chopped into ½-inch (12-mm) pieces

**Celery,** 1 stalk, thinly sliced

**Garlic,** 2 teaspoons finely chopped

**Vegetable broth,** 3 cups (24 fl oz/750 ml)

**Celery root,** 1 (about 14 oz/440 g), peeled and chopped into ½-inch (12-mm) pieces

**Large Yukon gold potato,** 1 (½ lb/250 g), peeled and cut into ½-inch (12-mm) pieces

**Dried savory or thyme,** 1 teaspoon

**Ground nutmeg,** ¼ teaspoon

**Sea salt and freshly ground pepper**

**Truffle oil,** for garnish (optional)

**Fresh chives,** 1 tablespoon finely chopped (optional)

**MAKES 4 SERVINGS**

1   In a large soup pot, warm the olive oil over medium heat. Add the onion, parsnip, and celery, and sauté until the onion is translucent, 5 minutes. Add the garlic and cook until aromatic, 30 seconds.

2   Add the broth, celery root, potato, savory, and 2 cups (16 fl oz/500 ml) water and bring to a boil over medium-high heat. Reduce the heat to low, cover, and simmer gently until the vegetables fall apart when pressed against the side of the pot, about 25 minutes.

3   Using an immersion blender, purée the soup until smooth, or blend it in batches in a blender with the lid slightly ajar to allow steam to escape. Pour the soup back into the pot and keep warm over low heat. Add the nutmeg and season to taste with salt and pepper. Divide among soup bowls and serve garnished with a drizzle of truffle oil and a sprinkle of chives, if using.

✄

Look for a celery root that has been trimmed of its diminutive stalks and leaves and has no mushy spots. To peel, start with a sharp vegetable peeler and then use a paring knife to trim out any crevices where dirt may be wedged, if necessary.

✄

Broccoli rabe looks like a leggy cousin of broccoli, but it's actually closer to a turnip green, with the same bitter, assertive bite. I mellow the rabe by blanching it and then pair it with nutty quinoa pasta.

# Quinoa Spaghetti with Broccoli Rabe, Feta, and Mint

**Broccoli rabe,** 1 lb (500 g)

**Quinoa or other whole-grain spaghetti,** ¾ lb (375 g)

**Extra-virgin olive oil,** ¼ cup (2 fl oz/ 60 ml)

**Garlic,** 6 large cloves, thinly sliced

**Red chile flakes,** 1 pinch

**Sea salt and freshly ground pepper**

**Crumbled feta cheese** (the softer and creamier, the better), 1 cup (4 oz/125 g)

**Walnuts,** 1 cup (4 oz/125 g), toasted and roughly chopped

**Fresh mint leaves,** ⅓ cup (⅓ oz/ 10 g) chopped

**MAKES 4 SERVINGS**

Choose broccoli rabe that has fresh—not split—stems, lots of green leaves, and deep green florets. Avoid bunches that have yellowing flowers or dry-looking stem ends.

1 Cut the broccoli rabe stems into bite-size lengths and set aside. Roughly chop the leaves and florets, keeping them separate from the stems. Bring a large pot of salted water to a boil. Add the stems to the water and boil for 1 minute. Add the leaves and florets to the water and boil until wilted and just tender, about 3 minutes. Using a fine-mesh sieve or slotted spoon, quickly remove the broccoli rabe from the cooking water and drain in a colander, shaking off any excess water still clinging to the leaves.

2 Return the cooking water to a boil, add the pasta, and cook according to package instructions.

3 While the pasta is cooking, in a large frying pan, warm the oil over medium heat. Add the garlic and sauté until aromatic, 1 minute. Add the reserved broccoli rabe and chile flakes, and sauté for 1 minute. Season with salt and pepper, then reduce the heat to low to keep warm.

4 When the pasta is ready, reserve ¾ cup (6 fl oz/180 ml) of the cooking water and drain the pasta. Add the pasta to the broccoli rabe in the frying pan along with the cheese, walnuts, and mint. Toss to combine the elements, adding as much of the reserved cooking water as needed to moisten the pasta. Serve right away.

These patties are full of exotic flavor thanks to curry paste and red jalapeño chiles. The patties freeze well, so you can have a healthy Indian meal at your fingertips. Spiced coconut rice has a great complementary flavor.

# Spinach-Chickpea Patties with Spiced Coconut Rice

You can freeze the cooked patties until firm, and then store them in the freezer in sealable plastic bags. Cook the frozen patties over low heat until heated through and crisp, about 8 minutes per side.

These patties are also delicious tucked into small burger buns and topped with mango chutney.

**Spiced Coconut Rice,** page 185

**Extra-virgin olive oil or coconut oil,** 2 tablespoons

**Yellow onion,** 1½ cups (7½ oz/235 g) finely chopped

**Red jalapeño chile,** 1, chopped

**Garlic,** 2 teaspoons finely chopped

**Baby spinach,** 2 cups (2 oz/60 g)

**Chickpeas,** 1 can (15 oz/470 g), drained and rinsed

**Panko bread crumbs,** ½ cup (½ oz/15 g)

**Fresh cilantro leaves,** 3 tablespoons

**Curry paste** (I like Patak's Mild Concentrated Curry Paste), 2 tablespoons

**Large egg,** 1, beaten

**Sea salt**

**Plain Greek yogurt,** ½ cup (4 oz/125 g) for serving

**MAKES 4 SERVINGS**

1 Follow the instructions on page 185 to make the rice. While the rice is cooking, in a large nonstick sauté pan, warm 1 tablespoon of the oil over medium heat. Add the onion and chile and sauté until the onion is caramelized, 8 minutes. Add the garlic and sauté until aromatic, 45 seconds.

3 Scrape the onion mixture into a food processor and set the pan aside. To the food processor, add the spinach, chickpeas, bread crumbs, cilantro, curry paste, egg, and ¼ teaspoon salt, and pulse until the beans and spinach are finely chopped. Let the mixture stand for 5 minutes; the bread crumbs will absorb some of the moisture and make the mixture easier to handle.

4 Warm the remaining 1 tablespoon oil in the sauté pan used to cook the onion mixture, and place it over medium heat. When the oil is shimmering, use an ice cream scoop to scoop up the bean mixture. Add it to the pan and press down to form a 3-inch (7.5-cm) patty. Repeat with the remaining bean mixture and fry until the patties are golden brown, 4 minutes per side. Watch carefully and reduce the heat if the patties begin to burn. Serve the patties with the rice and dollops of the yogurt.

In this vegetarian version of the famous Midwestern pizza, I use a purchased cornmeal crust and tofu-based Italian sausages. Keep this in mind for your busiest nights. Serve with a Caesar salad (hold the anchovy).

# Chicago-Style Pizza

**Prepared deep-dish cornmeal pizza crusts,** 2 (8- to 9-inches/20- to 23-cm in diameter)

**Part-skim mozzarella cheese,** 2 cups (8 oz/250 g) shredded

**Extra-virgin olive oil,** 1 tablespoon

**Vegetarian Italian sausages** (I like Tofurky brand), 3, cut into ½-inch (12-mm) slices

**Canned San Marzano tomatoes,** 1 cup (6 oz/185 g) drained and chopped

**Dried oregano,** 2 teaspoons

**Fennel seeds,** 1 teaspoon

**Parmesan cheese,** ½ cup (2 oz/60 g) grated

**MAKES 4 SERVINGS**

1   Preheat the oven to 425°F (220°C). Arrange the pizza crusts on 1 or 2 rimmed baking sheets. Top the pizza crusts evenly with the mozzarella cheese.

2   In a saucepan, warm the oil over medium heat. Add the sliced sausages and cook until crisped, 2 minutes per side. Transfer the sausage slices to the pizza crusts, dividing them evenly, then sprinkle with the tomatoes. Sprinkle the oregano and fennel seeds over the tomatoes, then finish by sprinkling each pizza with Parmesan cheese.

3   Bake the pizzas until the cheese is bubbly and the crust is golden brown underneath, about 10 minutes. Let the pizzas stand for a couple of minutes to cool slightly, then cut each pie into 4 wedges and serve.

For this recipe, I use Vicolo brand frozen cornmeal pizza crusts, but you can substitute your favorite prebaked crust. Just be sure it's at least ¼ inch (6 mm) deep, or the fillings may spill over the sides while baking.

This Tuscan-inspired soup acquires a simmered-for-hours flavor from a Parmesan cheese rind. I like to place the toast at the bottom of the bowl and ladle the soup over it, or you can serve it on the side for dipping.

# Cannellini Bean and Kale Soup with Garlic Toast

**Olive oil,** 2 tablespoons

**Yellow onion,** 1½ cups (7½ oz/235 g) finely chopped

**Carrot,** 1, peeled and finely chopped

**Celery,** 1 stalk, thinly sliced

**Fresh rosemary,** 2 teaspoons chopped

**Garlic,** 1 tablespoon finely chopped plus 1 whole peeled clove

**Cannellini beans,** 2 cans (each 15 oz/ 470 g), drained and rinsed

**Lacinato kale,** 4 cups (4 oz/125 g) chopped, stems and tough ribs removed

**Vegetable broth,** 2½ cups (20 fl oz/ 625 ml)

**Parmesan cheese rind,** 1 piece (3 inch/7.5 cm)

**Whole-grain bread,** ½ loaf (8 oz/250 g)

**Sea salt and freshly ground pepper**

**MAKES 4 SERVINGS**

Save the rinds from Parmesan cheese in a sealable plastic bag in the refrigerator for up to 3 months to add them to soups, stews, pasta sauces, and pots of beans. You can find just the rinds for sale at some cheese shops and grocery stores with a well-stocked cheese department. Some shops will even give them away, so it pays to ask!

1 Preheat the oven to 400°F (200°C). In a large soup pot, warm 1 tablespoon of the oil over medium heat. Add the onion, carrot, celery, and rosemary, and sauté until the onion is translucent, 5 minutes. Add the chopped garlic and sauté until aromatic, 45 seconds.

2 Add the beans, kale, broth, and cheese rind and bring to a simmer. Cover and cook until the vegetables are tender, 18 minutes.

3 Meanwhile, make the garlic toasts: Rub the reserved whole garlic clove all over the bread, then discard the clove. Slice the bread into 4 slices (each ¼ inch/6 mm thick) and arrange them on a rimmed baking sheet. Brush with the remaining 1 tablespoon oil and bake until golden brown, about 10 minutes.

4 Season the soup to taste with salt and pepper. Place a garlic toast in the bottom of 4 shallow soup bowls and ladle the soup over the toasts, discarding the cheese rind. Serve right away.

(V) Nutritional yeast gives the pan-fried tofu in this easy stir-fry a nutty, savory flavor. The sweet, mildly spicy sauce keeps for up to 2 weeks in the refrigerator, so consider making a double batch for a future meal.

# Crispy Orange Tofu with Broccoli

**Extra-firm tofu,** 1 lb (500 g)

**Canola oil,** 2 tablespoons

**Tamari,** 2 tablespoons

**Nutritional yeast,** 1 tablespoon

**Cornstarch,** 2 teaspoons

**Freshly squeezed orange juice,** ⅓ cup (3 fl oz/80 ml)

**Sweet red chile sauce** (I like Mae Ploy brand), 2 tablespoons

**Dark sesame oil,** 1 tablespoon

**Garlic,** 1 tablespoon finely chopped

**Fresh ginger,** 1 tablespoon finely chopped

**Broccoli florets,** ½ lb (250 g), cut into 1½-inch (4-cm) pieces

**Small red bell pepper,** 1, seeded and cut into ½-inch (12-mm) strips

**Steamed brown jasmine rice,** for serving

**MAKES 4 SERVINGS**

Nutritional yeast (also labeled brewer's yeast) comes in both large flake and finely ground varieties. This recipe works best with finely ground nutritional yeast. You can also try it sprinkled on popcorn, or stirred into sauces to add a slightly salty, nutty flavor.

1 Drain the tofu, wrap it in paper towels, place a heavy plate on top, and let stand for 10 minutes to press out excess liquid. Cut the pressed tofu into 1-inch (2.5-cm) cubes. In a nonstick frying pan, warm 1½ teaspoons of the canola oil over medium-high heat. Add the tofu and cook, turning occasionally, until golden brown all over, 10 minutes; remove from the pan.

2 Return the pan to medium-high and add 1½ teaspoons canola oil. Return the tofu to the pan and sprinkle it with 2 teaspoons of the tamari and the nutritional yeast. Cook, reducing the heat if necessary, and turning with tongs occasionally, until the tofu is coated and crispy, 2 minutes. Set aside.

3 Put the cornstarch in a small bowl. Gradually whisk in the remaining 4 teaspoons tamari, the orange juice, chile sauce, and sesame oil.

4 In a wok or large, deep sauté pan, warm the remaining 1 tablespoon canola oil over medium-high heat. Add the garlic and ginger and stir-fry until aromatic, 20 seconds. Add the broccoli and bell pepper and stir-fry until the broccoli is bright green, 2 minutes. Add 2 tablespoons water, cover, and steam until the broccoli is crisp-tender, 2 minutes. Uncover the wok, add the orange juice mixture, and stir-fry until the sauce is bubbly, 1 minute. Fold in the tofu. Serve right away with the rice.

Brown lentils take the place of beef in this hearty winter soup, while dried porcini mushrooms add deep flavor and meaty texture. I like to serve this soup with dark rye bread and a crisp romaine salad with hardboiled eggs.

# Beet and Lentil Borscht

**Dried porcini mushrooms,** ½ oz (15 g)

**Boiling water,** 1 cup (8 fl oz/250 ml)

**Olive oil,** 1 tablespoon

**Yellow onion,** 1½ cups (7½ oz/235 g) finely chopped

**Carrots,** 2, peeled and finely chopped

**Celery,** 1 stalk, thinly sliced

**Garlic,** 2 teaspoons minced

**Red beets,** ¾ lb (375 g), peeled and cut into ½-inch (12-mm) cubes (about 3 medium beets)

**Vegetable broth,** 4 cups (32 fl oz/1 l)

**Large Yukon gold potato,** 1, peeled and cut into ½-inch (12-mm) cubes

**Dried brown lentils,** ¾ cup (5¼ oz/ 160 g)

**Dried bay leaf,** 1

**Dried dill,** 2 teaspoons

**Ground allspice,** ¼ teaspoon

**Tomato paste,** 2 tablespoons

**Red wine vinegar,** 2 tablespoons

**Sea salt and freshly ground pepper**

**Sour cream,** for garnish

MAKES 4—6 SERVINGS

When handling the beets, you may wish to wear plastic gloves to keep them from staining your hands. If you're short on time, you can pick up roasted-and-peeled beets in the produce section of specialty food stores and some supermarkets and cut them into cubes. Add them to the soup during the last 15 minutes of simmering in step 2.

1 In a small, heatproof bowl, place the dried mushrooms. Pour the boiling water on top and let stand until softened, 15 minutes. Using a slotted spoon, remove and drain the mushrooms. Chop the mushrooms and reserve the soaking liquid.

2 In a large soup pot, warm the oil over medium heat. Add the onion, carrots, and celery, and sauté until tender, 5 minutes. Add the garlic and sauté until aromatic, 45 seconds. Add the porcini mushrooms, the reserved soaking water (avoid the sediment in the bottom of the bowl), the beets, broth, potato, lentils, bay leaf, dill, allspice, and 1½ cups (12 fl oz/375 ml) water. Bring to a simmer, cover, then reduce heat to medium-low. Simmer until the beets, potatoes, and lentils are just tender, 30 minutes.

3 Ladle ½ cup (4 fl oz/125 ml) of the soup liquid into a small bowl, whisk in the tomato paste, and return the mixture to the pot. Simmer for 5 minutes. Add the vinegar and season to taste with salt and pepper. Divide the soup among bowls and serve with dollops of sour cream.

(V) This mix of Cajun-style seasoned rice, collards, and black-eyed peas, also called Hoppin' John, is delicious anytime. It's traditionally eaten on New Year's Day, and is said to guarantee prosperity for the coming year.

# Rice Pilaf with Collard Greens and Black-Eyed Peas

Collard greens can be a bit unwieldy on the cutting board. To make the leaves easier to chop, stack them, roll them up tightly, and thinly slice the roll crosswise into thin ribbons.

✕

If you want a heartier meal, add a few links of sautéed vegetarian sausage to the rice and serve it with warm corn bread (page 185) slathered with honey butter.

**Extra-virgin olive oil,** 2 tablespoons

**Yellow onion,** 1½ cups (7½ oz/235 g) finely chopped

**Celery,** 3 stalks, thinly sliced

**Green bell pepper,** 1, seeded and chopped

**Garlic,** 1 tablespoon finely chopped

**Collard greens,** ½ bunch, tough ribs discarded, leaves chopped (about 4 cups/4 oz/125 g)

**Long-grain white rice,** 1 cup (7 oz/220 g)

**Cajun seasoning,** 1 tablespoon

**Vegetable broth,** 2½ cups (20 fl oz/ 625 ml)

**Frozen black-eyed peas,** 1¼ cups (6 oz/195 g)

**Hot-pepper sauce,** for serving

**MAKES 4 SERVINGS**

1 In a large sauté pan with a lid, warm the oil over medium heat. Add the onion, celery, and bell pepper and sauté until the onion is translucent, 6 minutes. Add the garlic and cook until aromatic, 45 seconds. Add the greens and cook, stirring frequently, until the greens are wilted, 2 minutes.

2 Add the rice and Cajun seasoning and stir until the rice is coated with oil. Add the broth and stir well. Sprinkle the black-eyed peas over the top of the rice mixture without stirring them in. Bring the liquid to a simmer, cover, and cook over low heat until the rice has absorbed all the liquid, 25 minutes.

3 Transfer the mixture to a serving dish and serve right away, passing the hot sauce at the table for diners to season to their own preference.

(V) Soothing Japanese "hot pot" soups are served directly from the pot at the table. Though they often contain meat or seafood, there are also soulful vegetarian soups like this one that rely on fried tofu and vegetables.

# Japanese Hot Pot with Tofu

**Cellophane noodles** (bean thread noodles), 2 cups (1½ oz/45 g)

**Vegetarian dashi or konbu-shiitake stock (see page 47),** 4 cups (32 oz/1 l)

**White miso,** ½ cup (4 oz/125 g)

**Mirin** (sweet Japanese cooking wine), ⅓ cup (3 fl oz/80 ml)

**Napa cabbage,** ¼ head (about 2 cups/6 oz/185 g) chopped

**Fried tofu,** ½ lb (250 g), cut into 8 slabs, each ¼-inch (6-mm) thick

**Oyster or stemmed shiitake mushrooms,** ¼ lb (125 g), roughly chopped

**Carrot,** 1, peeled and thinly sliced

**Baby bok choy,** 1 head, cut crosswise into 1-inch (2.5-cm) slices

**Green onions,** 4, thinly sliced

**Soy sauce**

**MAKES 4 SERVINGS**

1 In a large bowl, cover the noodles with cold water and let them soak until pliable, 20 minutes.

2 Drain the noodles. Cut the noodles into 2-inch (5-cm) lengths and set aside. In a large bowl, whisk together the dashi, miso, and mirin; set aside.

3 Place the cabbage in a large saucepan. Arrange the tofu, mushrooms, carrot, and bok choy on top of the cabbage in separate piles around the edges of the pot, then place the noodles in the center. Gently pour the broth mixture over the ingredients in the pot, and bring to a boil over high heat. Reduce the heat to low, cover, and simmer until the vegetables are just tender, 5 minutes.

4 Sprinkle the soup with the green onions and season the broth to taste with soy sauce. Set out chop sticks, soup spoons, and individual serving bowls at the table. Serve the soup at the table from the pot.

Traditional dashi broth is a Japanese staple made from sea kelp (konbu) and smoked dried tuna flakes (bonito). You can make vegetarian dashi broth from scratch by simmering konbu and dried shiitake mushrooms (see page 47), or you can use instant vegetarian dashi powder (available at Asian markets and online), which is an invaluable staple for vegetarian cooking.

Garnet yams make a delicious and healthy alternative to regular white potatoes. In this satisfying main-dish recipe, they are baked twice and stuffed with spinach, provolone cheese, and spiced pecans.

# Garnet Yams Stuffed with Greens, Cheese, and Pecans

**Large garnet yams,** 4 (each about ¾ lb/ 375 g)

**White (shiro) miso,** 2 tablespoons

**Provolone or cheddar cheese,** 1 cup (4 oz/125 g) grated

**Extra-virgin olive oil,** 2 teaspoons

**Baby spinach,** 4 cups packed (6 oz/ 185 g)

**Sea salt and freshly ground pepper**

**Pecans,** 1 cup (4 oz/125 g) roughly chopped

**Unsalted butter,** 2 tablespoons, melted

**Brown sugar,** 4 teaspoons firmly packed

**Fresh rosemary,** 2 teaspoons chopped

**Cayenne pepper,** ⅛ teaspoon

**MAKES 4 SERVINGS**

Garnet yams have mahogany skins that yield bright orange flesh. They are not interchangeable with pale-skinned sweet potatoes, which tend to have a much drier flesh and are significantly less sweet.

1 Preheat the oven to 350°F (180°C). Prick the yams all over with a fork, then bake them until tender, 45 minutes to 1 hour. (Alternatively, after pricking them, place the yams on a paper towel and microwave them on high, turning once or twice, until they yield easily when squeezed, 10—15 minutes.)

2 Cut a long slit down the length of the yams. Using a sturdy spoon, scoop out the centers, leaving a ½-inch (12-mm) shell. Transfer the scooped-out flesh to a large bowl. Add the miso and cheese to the bowl, and, using a potato masher, mash until mostly smooth.

3 In a sauté pan, warm the oil over medium heat. Add the spinach and sauté until wilted, 3 minutes. Transfer the mixture to the bowl with the mashed yams and stir to combine; season to taste with salt and pepper. Spoon the mixture into the yam skins.

4 In a small bowl, combine the pecans, butter, brown sugar, rosemary, cayenne, ½ teaspoon salt, and ¼ teaspoon pepper. Sprinkle the nut mixture on top of the yams. Transfer the yams to a baking sheet and bake until the tops are golden brown, 25 minutes. Let the stuffed yams cool for a few minutes and serve.

I learned to make this savory pie in Greece, where it is typically stuffed with a mix of wild greens called horta. At home, I use greens that are in season; in winter, that means chard and kale, along with hothouse spinach.

# Mixed Greens Spanikopita

**Extra-virgin olive oil,** 3 tablespoons

**Garlic,** 1 teaspoon minced

**Swiss chard,** 1 bunch, leaves torn, tough ribs and stems discarded

**Kale,** 1 bunch, leaves torn, tough ribs and stems discarded

**Baby spinach,** 6 oz (185 g)

**Creamy feta cheese,** 1½ cups (7 oz/220 g) crumbled

**Fresh dill,** ½ cup (½ oz/15 g) chopped

**Green onions,** 4, thinly sliced

**Sea salt and freshly ground pepper**

**Large eggs,** 4, beaten

**Unsalted butter,** 2 tablespoons, melted

**Frozen filo dough,** 8 sheets, thawed according to package instructions

**Pine nuts,** ¼ cup (1 oz/30 g)

**MAKES 4—6 SERVINGS**

Some natural food stores carry a cleaned and chopped "braising greens mix," which is usually a blend of different types of kale, chard, and collards. This mixture can be substituted for the chard and kale in this recipe; you will need about 14 cups (14 oz/440 g) total.

✻

You get what you pay for with feta cheese. Dry, salty feta crumbles won't work here. I recommend softer, slightly creamy feta cheese for this recipe, available where artisan cheeses are sold.

1 In a large, deep sauté pan, warm 1 tablespoon of the oil over medium-high heat. Add the garlic and sauté for about 20 seconds. Add the chard and kale and cook, tossing constantly with tongs, until tender, 4 minutes. Add the spinach and cook until tender, 1½ minutes. Transfer the mixture to a fine-mesh sieve and, using a spatula, press the greens to extract as much liquid as is possible. In a large bowl, combine the greens with the cheese, dill, and green onions. Season with salt and pepper. Add the eggs and mix well.

2 Preheat the oven to 350°F (180°C). In a small bowl, combine the butter and remaining 2 tablespoons oil. Brush a 9-inch (23-cm) pie pan with the butter mixture. Place 2 sheets of filo on a work surface; cover the remaining filo with a towel. Pick up the right half of the top sheet of filo as if you were turning the page of a book and brush the sheet beneath it with the butter mixture. Return the lifted portion down to the sheet underneath it, then repeat with left side of the filo. Brush the top sheet with the butter mixture and place the stack in the pie dish. Repeat this process 3 more times, layering the filo sheets in the pie dish facing different directions so that the edges hang 2–3 inches (5–7.5 cm) over the pan's circumference.

3 Transfer the greens mixture to the pie pan, sprinkle it with the pine nuts, and fold the overhanging filo loosely over the top. Brush the top with the remaining butter mixture and bake until the filo is deep golden brown, 35—40 minutes. Cut into wedges and serve.

Called "sambar" in India, this stew is at once filling and healthy. The sweetness of the vegetables is tempered by the tart tamarind paste that is stirred into the soup after cooking. I serve the soup with warm, puffy flatbread.

# South Indian–Style Lentil and Vegetable Stew

**Dried red lentils,** ½ cup (3½ oz/105 g), picked over and rinsed

**Curry powder,** 1½ teaspoons

**Ground coriander,** 1 teaspoon

**Sea salt**

**Sweet potato,** 1, peeled and cut into ½-inch (12-mm) cubes

**Small Japanese eggplant,** 1, cut into ½-inch (12-mm) cubes

**Carrot,** 1, peeled and chopped

**Frozen okra,** 1 cup (4 oz/125 g), chopped

**Garlic naan bread** (I like Stonefire's garlic naan), ¾ lb (375 g)

**Unsalted butter,** 2 tablespoons

**Brown mustard seeds,** 1 teaspoon

**Cumin seeds,** ½ teaspoon

**Fresh or frozen curry leaves** (optional), ¼ cup

**Garlic,** 1 tablespoon finely chopped

**Tamarind concentrate** (such as Tamicon), 2 teaspoons

**Cayenne pepper**

**MAKES 4 SERVINGS**

How fresh is the curry powder in your pantry? If you've had it for over a year, or it doesn't smell fragrant as soon as you open the jar, discard it and replace it with only as much as you can use quickly.

✄

Look for tamarind paste and fresh curry leaves at Indian markets and some specialty food stores.

✄

You can also serve this stew with warm basmati rice instead of the naan.

1 Preheat the oven to 400°F (200°C). In a saucepan, place the lentils, curry powder, coriander, and 1 teaspoon salt. Stir in 4 cups (32 fl oz/1 l) water and bring to a boil, stirring frequently to make sure the lentils don't stick to the bottom of the pan. When the liquid is boiling, add the sweet potato, eggplant, carrot, and okra, and reduce the heat to medium-low. Simmer, uncovered, until the vegetables are tender and the lentils are falling apart, 15–20 minutes.

2 While the soup is simmering, warm the bread in the oven for 10 minutes. Wrap in foil to keep warm until ready to eat.

3 In a small sauté pan, melt the butter over medium heat. Add the mustard and cumin seeds and cook until the seeds begin to pop, 20 seconds. Add the curry leaves, if using, and garlic and sauté until aromatic, 30 seconds. Scrape the spiced butter into the stew and stir to mix. Stir in the tamarind and season to taste with salt and cayenne. Serve hot with the warm naan bread.

(V) This Korean soup stars soft tofu, zucchini, cabbage, and red chile kimchi. You can adjust the spiciness of the soup by purchasing mild kimchi and using less chile paste, if desired. Serve with hot steamed rice.

# Tofu Kimchi Stew

**Canola oil,** 1 tablespoon

**Yellow onion,** ½, thinly sliced

**Napa cabbage kimchi,** 1 cup (4 oz/ 120 g) roughly chopped, plus ½ cup (4 fl oz/125 ml) juice from kimchi jar

**Garlic,** 2 teaspoons finely chopped

**Fresh ginger,** 2 teaspoons finely chopped

**Vegetable broth,** 2 cups (16 fl oz/ 500 ml)

**Small zucchini,** 1, halved lengthwise and sliced into ¼-inch (6-mm) pieces

**Mirin,** ¼ cup (2 fl oz/60 ml)

**Gochujang or sambal oelek chile paste** (optional), 1—2 tablespoons

**Sugar,** 1 teaspoon

**Soft tofu,** ½ lb (250 g)

**Soy sauce,** 1—2 tablespoons

**Dark sesame oil,** 1 teaspoon

**Green onions,** 3 tablespoons thinly sliced

**MAKES 4 SERVINGS**

1 In a large saucepan, warm the canola oil over medium heat. Add the onion and cook until it begins to brown, 4 minutes. Add the chopped kimchi, garlic, and ginger, and cook for 2 minutes.

2 Add the broth, zucchini, mirin, chile paste (if using), sugar, 2 cups (16 fl oz/ 500 ml) water, and the reserved kimchi juice, and bring to a simmer. Cover and cook until the zucchini is tender, 10 minutes. Break up the tofu into 1-inch (2.5-cm) pieces and gently stir it into the soup. Cook until heated through, 5 minutes.

3 Taste the broth—it should be spicy, sweet, and a little sour from the kimchi. Adjust the seasoning to taste with soy sauce and additional chile paste, if desired. Stir in the sesame oil, ladle the soup into the bowls, sprinkle with the green onions, and serve.

✕

Gochujang is a spicy-sweet red condiment made from red chiles and fermented beans. The thick paste is used extensively in Korean cuisine as a condiment for everything from grilled tofu to soup. You'll usually find it sold in small plastic tubs at Asian markets or online. I'm partial to Annie Chun's gochujang because it is not too hot and it in comes in a convenient 10-ounce (315-g) bottle.

✕

Whenever I need a dose of sunshine in the coldest winter months, I make these Jamaican black bean and quinoa patties. The spicy-sweet mango salsa makes a wonderful counterpoint to the spiced cakes.

# Quinoa–Black Bean Cakes with Mango-Avocado Salsa

**Quinoa,** ½ cup (4 oz/115 g), rinsed and drained

**Coconut milk,** ½ cup (4 fl oz/125 ml)

**Salt-free Jamaican jerk seasoning,** 2 teaspoons

**Sea salt**

**Garnet yam or sweet potato,** ⅓ lb (155 g), peeled and cut into ½-inch (12-mm) cubes

**Black beans,** 1 can (15 oz/425 g), rinsed and drained

**Red bell pepper,** ½ cup (2½ oz/75 g) finely chopped

**Panko bread crumbs,** ½ cup (½ oz/15 g)

**Green onions,** 2, thinly sliced

**Habanero hot sauce,** 1 tablespoon

**Large egg,** 1, beaten

**Extra-virgin olive oil,** 1 tablespoon

**Mango-Avocado Salsa,** page 186

**MAKES 4 SERVINGS**

1 In a small saucepan, combine the quinoa, coconut milk, and jerk seasoning with ¼ teaspoon salt and ¼ cup (2 fl oz/60 ml) water, and bring to a boil over medium-high heat. Reduce the heat to low, cover, and simmer, stirring once or twice, until all the liquid has been absorbed, 20 minutes.

2 Meanwhile, place the yam in a small saucepan and add enough water to just cover. Add a large pinch of salt. Bring to a boil over medium heat, then simmer until tender, 5—8 minutes. Drain.

3 In a large bowl, combine the quinoa mixture, yams, black beans, bell peppers, panko, green onions, and hot sauce. Using a potato masher, mash until most of the yams and beans are mashed. Stir in the egg and let the mixture stand for 5 minutes; in that time, the bread crumbs will absorb some of the moisture and make the mixture easier to handle.

4 In a large nonstick frying pan, warm the oil over medium heat. Using a 1 cup (8 fl oz/250 ml) measure, scoop up the bean mixture, place it in the pan, and press down with a spatula or your fingertips to make a 4-inch (10-cm) cake that is about 1 inch (2.5 cm) thick. Repeat with the remaining bean mixture to make 4 cakes. Reduce the heat to medium-low and cook until crisp on the outside and heated through, 5 minutes per side. Serve with the salsa.

Jerk seasoning is an earthy, sometimes fiery blend of allspice, chiles, cloves, cumin, and often a lot of salt. I prefer to use salt-free jerk seasoning blend, like Spice Hunter brand. Look for it at natural food stores and online. Try it as a seasoning for grilled, buttered corn on the cob.

If you like, you can cook the yams in the microwave: In a small microwave-safe bowl, combine the yams with ¼ cup (2 fl oz/60 ml) water. Cover and cook on high until the yams are soft when pierced with a fork, 4 minutes. Drain well.

This lean version of broccoli-cheese soup gets its creamy texture (and ample protein) from cannellini beans. Be sure to whisk the cheese into the soup gradually, off of the heat, so that it melts smoothly.

# Broccoli and Cheddar Soup

**Unsalted butter,** 2 tablespoons

**Leeks,** 2 cups (6 oz/185 g) thinly sliced (about 1 large leek), white and pale green parts only

**Garlic,** 1 tablespoon finely chopped

**Broccoli crowns,** 1½ lb (750 g), chopped (about 7 cups)

**Sea salt and freshly ground pepper**

**Vegetable broth,** 4 cups (32 fl oz/1 l) mild

**Cannellini beans,** 1 can (14 oz/400 g), drained and rinsed

**Dry mustard powder,** 1½ teaspoons

**Sharp Cheddar cheese,** 1½ cups (6 oz/185 g) shredded, at room temperature

**Freshly grated nutmeg,** ¼ teaspoon

**MAKES 4 SERVINGS**

1 In a large soup pot, melt the butter over medium-low heat. Add the leeks and sauté until tender but not browned, 4 minutes. Add the garlic and cook until aromatic, 45 seconds. Add the broccoli and a generous pinch of salt and sauté until bright-green and aromatic, 4 minutes.

2 Add the broth, beans, and mustard powder and bring to a boil over medium-high heat. Reduce the heat to low, cover, and simmer until the broccoli is fall-apart tender, 20 minutes.

3 In batches, blend the soup in a blender with the lid slightly ajar, or use an immersion blender to blend the soup in the pot off the heat.

4 Return the soup to the pot. Off of the heat, gradually whisk the cheese into the soup and stir until melted. Add the nutmeg and season to taste with salt and pepper. Serve right away.

Before you begin the soup, take the cheese out of the refrigerator to come to room temperature; it will melt more easily when added to the soup.

✕

Broccoli crowns are trimmed so there are more florets and less woody stems than in a natural bunch. If you can't find crowns, trim the thick broccoli stems with a paring knife so you're left with the tender, near-white cores. Chop them finely before adding them to the soup.

✕

The soup is best immediately after it has been cooked. If there are leftovers, you can reheat the soup in a small saucepan over very low heat (just make sure not to bring it to a simmer or the cheese may curdle). You can also reheat it gently in the microwave on 50% power.

This rich pasta dish is a vegetarian riff on a Hungarian paprika-infused chicken dish. I like to serve it on wide, fresh pasta ribbons, but dried egg noodles or spaetzle (page 185) would also be wonderful.

# Creamy Mushroom Paprikash Over Pasta

**Unsalted butter,** 3 tablespoons

**Cremini mushrooms,** 1 lb (500 g), quartered

**Caraway seeds,** ½ teaspoon

**Sea salt and freshly ground pepper**

**Yellow onion,** 2 cups (7 oz/220 g) thinly sliced

**Tomato paste,** 2 tablespoons

**Sweet Hungarian paprika,** 1 teaspoon

**Dry white wine,** ¾ cup (6 fl oz/180 ml)

**Fresh pappardelle pasta,** ¾ lb (375 g)

**Sour cream or crème fraîche,** ½ cup (4 fl oz/125 ml)

**Fresh dill,** ¼ cup (¼ oz/7 g) chopped

**MAKES 4 SERVINGS**

✂

Don't overcrowd the mushrooms or they will sweat and steam without properly browning. I use a 14-inch (35-cm) cast-iron frying pan for the job. You can also sauté the mushrooms in batches in a smaller pan.

✂

1 Bring a large pot of salted water to a boil. Meanwhile, in a wide frying pan over medium heat, melt 2 tablespoons of the butter. Add the mushrooms, caraway seeds, and ½ teaspoon salt, and sauté until the mushrooms release their liquid and begin to brown, 8 minutes.

2 Add the onion and sauté until the onion is tender and browned, 5 minutes. Stir in the tomato paste and paprika and cook for 1 minute. Reduce the heat to medium, add the wine, and simmer until about half the liquid has evaporated and the sauce has thickened, 2 minutes. Cover and set aside.

3 Add the pasta to the boiling water and cook until al dente according to the package instructions. Reserve ½ cup (4 fl oz/125 ml) of the cooking liquid and drain the pasta. Place the pasta in a large serving bowl and toss with the remaining 1 tablespoon butter. Fold the sour cream and dill into the mushroom sauce and season to taste with salt and pepper, adding a bit of the pasta cooking liquid to moisten, if necessary. Spoon the sauce over the pasta and serve right away.

Rösti are crisp, pan-fried potato cakes from Switzerland. I like to add a root vegetable, like the beets here, to mine for flavor and nutrients. Serve the rösti topped with poached eggs for a perfect breakfast-for-dinner meal.

# Potato and Beet Rösti with Poached Eggs

**Yukon gold potatoes,** 1 lb (500 g)

**Golden beets,** ½ lb (250 g), peeled

**Truffle salt,** ¾ teaspoon

**Sea salt and freshly ground pepper**

**Unsalted butter,** 3 tablespoons

**Large eggs,** 4, poached (page 186)

**Fresh chives,** 2 tablespoons finely chopped

**MAKES 4 SERVINGS**

1 Preheat the oven to 200°F (95°C). Bring a saucepan of water to a boil. Add the unpeeled potatoes and boil until softened, 7 minutes. Drain and let cool for 5 minutes. Shred the potatoes on the large holes of a box grater or in a food processor with the shredding disk, then shred the raw beets the same way. Transfer the shredded vegetables to a large bowl and season with the truffle salt and ½ teaspoon pepper.

2 Spray a 10-inch (25-cm) nonstick sauté pan with cooking spray. Place the pan over medium heat and add 2 tablespoons of the butter. When the butter is melted, add the vegetable mixture to the pan, pressing down with a spatula to compress it into a neat cake. Reduce the heat to medium-low, cover, and cook for 5 minutes. Uncover and cook until the cake is golden brown on the bottom, about 5 minutes. Using a spatula, loosen the edges of the cake. Place a plate on top of the pan, and, using oven mitts, carefully invert the cake onto the plate. Return the pan to medium-low heat and add the remaining 1 tablespoon butter. Transfer the cake to the pan cooked side up and continue to cook until crisp and golden on the bottom, 8—10 minutes. Place in the oven to keep warm.

4 Follow the instructions on page 186 to poach the eggs. While the eggs are poaching, remove the rösti from the oven and cut it into 4 wedges. Divide the wedges among 4 plates. When the eggs are ready, remove them from the poaching liquid using a slotted spoon, and pat them dry with paper towels. Top each rösti wedge with a poached egg. Sprinkle with salt, pepper, and chives and serve right away.

The rösti can be made up to 3 hours ahead of time and reheated in a 350°F (180°C) oven for 10 minutes.

# Basic Recipes

The following recipes appear throughout the book as elements of larger recipes or are staples that can be used for vegetarian meals anytime.

## Herbed Crepes

**Whole milk,** ¾ cup (6 fl oz/180 ml) plus 2 tablespoons

**Large eggs,** 2

**Fresh tarragon,** 1½ teaspoons chopped

**Sea salt,** ¾ teaspoon

**All-purpose flour,** ¾ cup (4¼ oz/120 g)

**Unsalted butter,** 2 tablespoons, melted

In a bowl, whisk together the milk, eggs, tarragon, and salt. Add the flour and blend just until smooth. Stir in the butter; set aside while you make the crepe filling.

When you're ready to cook, warm an 8-inch (20-cm) nonstick frying pan over medium heat. Spray with cooking spray, lift the pan off the heat, and add ¼ cup (2 fl oz/60 ml) of the batter, swirling the pan so the batter coats the bottom evenly. Return to the heat and cook until the edges of the crepe begin to dry and the bottom is golden in spots, 30 seconds. Flip the crepe and cook on second side, 30 seconds. Wrap the crepe in foil and keep warm while cooking the 7 remaining crepes. You may need to reduce the heat as the pan heats up so the crepes do not burn; add more cooking spray as needed if the crepes begin to stick to the pan.

**MAKES 8 CREPES**

## Pizza Dough

**All-purpose flour,** 1 cup (5 oz/155 g), plus more for rolling

**Whole-wheat flour,** 1 cup (5 oz/155 g)

**Instant yeast,** 1 envelope

**Sugar,** 1 teaspoon

**Sea salt,** ½ teaspoon

**Warm water** (120°F/52°C), 1 cup (8 fl oz/250 ml)

**Extra-virgin olive oil,** 2 tablespoons, plus more for brushing

In a stand mixer fitted with the dough hook, combine the 1 cup (5 oz/155 g) all-purpose flour with the whole-wheat flour, yeast, sugar, and salt. Add the water and 2 tablespoons of the olive oil and stir until blended. Mix on medium speed until the dough is smooth and elastic, 4–8 minutes. Cover and let the dough rest for 10–30 minutes.

**MAKES 1 LB (500 G) DOUGH**

## Whole Wheat Galette Dough

**Whole-wheat flour,** ¾ cup (4 oz/125 g)

**Fine yellow cornmeal,** ¼ cup (1¼ oz/35 g)

**Sea salt**

**Unsalted butter,** ⅓ cup (3 oz/90 g), cut into ½-inch (12-mm) cubes

**Chilled buttermilk,** ¼ cup (2 fl oz/60 ml) plus 1 tablespoon

In a food processor, pulse the flour, cornmeal, and ½ teaspoon salt. Add the butter and pulse until the butter forms coarse crumbs, about 15 pulses. Add the buttermilk and pulse just until the dough just comes together. Form the dough into an 8-inch (20-cm) disk, wrap it in plastic wrap, and freeze for 10 minutes.

**MAKES DOUGH FOR ONE 10-INCH (25-CM) GALETTE**

## Masa Dough for Sopes

**Masa harina,** 1½ cups (8¼ oz/260 g)

**Chili powder,** 1 teaspoon

**Sea salt,** ½ teaspoon

**Warm water** (120°F/49°C), 1 cup (8 fl oz/250 ml)

In a bowl, whisk the masa harina, chili powder, and salt. Add the warm water and knead until the dough is smooth and no longer sticky. Divide the dough into 12 golf ball–size pieces. Cover with plastic wrap and set aside for 10 minutes.

**MAKES DOUGH FOR 12 SOPES**

## Herbed Biscuit Dough

**Whole-wheat pastry flour,** 2 cups (10 oz/285 g)

**Fresh mixed herbs such as rosemary, thyme, and sage,** 1 tablespoon chopped

**Baking powder,** 2 teaspoons

**Sea salt,** ½ teaspoon

**Cold unsalted butter,** ⅓ cup (3 oz/90 g) cut into ½-inch (12-mm) cubes

**Milk,** ⅔ cup (5 fl oz/160 ml)

**Grated Parmesan cheese,** ½ cup (2 oz/55 g)

Place the flour, herbs, baking powder, and salt in a food processor or mixing bowl and pulse or whisk to combine. Add the butter and pulse or cut it into the flour with a pastry blender until the butter is finely crumbled. Add the milk and cheese and pulse or stir until the mixture just comes together. Use right away.

**MAKES DOUGH FOR 8 BISCUITS**

## Spaetzle Batter

**Large eggs,** 3

**Milk,** ¼ cup (2 fl oz/60 ml) plus 2 tablespoons

**Mixed fresh herbs,** 2 tablespoons finely chopped

**Sea salt,** ¾ teaspoon

**Freshly ground pepper,** ½ teaspoon

**All-purpose flour,** 1½ cups (7½ oz/235 g)

In a bowl with a spout, whisk together the eggs, milk, mixed herbs, salt, and pepper. Stir in the flour until the mixture is the consistency of thick pancake batter. Pour the batter into a plastic squeeze bottle with a ¼-inch (6-mm) hole in the tip. Use right away.

**MAKES DOUGH FOR 4 SERVINGS OF SPAETZLE**

## Masa Dumpling Dough

**Masa harina,** ½ cup (2¾ oz/80 g)

**All-purpose flour,** ¼ cup (1½ oz/45 g)

**Baking powder,** ½ teaspoon

**Sea salt,** ½ teaspoon

**Unsalted butter,** 1 tablespoon, cut into small pieces

**Milk,** 6 tablespoons (3 fl oz/90 ml), or more as needed

**Fresh cilantro,** 1 tablespoon finely chopped

In a bowl, whisk together the masa harina, flour, baking powder, and salt. Using your fingertips, rub the butter into the flour mixture until finely crumbled. Add the milk and cilantro and stir gently until the dough comes together. (If the dough seems dry, add a little more milk, 1 teaspoon at a time.)

**MAKES DOUGH FOR ABOUT 18 DUMPLINGS**

## Spiced Coconut Rice

**Unsalted butter,** 1 tablespoon

**Ginger,** 1 tablespoon finely chopped

**Cardamom pods,** 4

**Whole cloves,** 4

**Cinnamon stick,** 1, broken in half

**Coconut milk,** 1¼ cups (10 fl oz/310 ml)

**Turmeric,** ¼ teaspoon

**Sea salt,** ½ teaspoon

**Long-grain white Rice,** 1½ cups (10½ oz/470 g), rinsed

In a saucepan, warm the butter over medium heat. Add the ginger, cardamom, cloves, and cinnamon and sauté until aromatic, 30 seconds. Add the coconut milk, turmeric, salt and 1⅓ cups (11 fl oz/360 ml) water and bring to a boil. Add the rice, bring back to a simmer, cover partially, and reduce the heat to low. Simmer for 12 minutes, then remove from the heat and let the rice stand for 10 minutes.

**MAKES 4 SERVINGS**

## Corn Bread

**All purpose flour,** 1 cup (5 oz/155 g)

**Cornmeal,** 1 cup (5 oz/155 g)

**Sugar,** ⅓ cup (3 oz/90 g)

**Baking powder,** 1 tablespoon

**Sea salt,** ½ teaspoon

**Milk,** ¾ cup (6 fl oz/180 ml)

**Sour cream,** ½ cup (4 oz/125 g)

**Large eggs,** 2

**Unsalted butter,** 3 tablespoons, melted

Preheat the oven to 350°F (180°C). In a bowl, whisk together the flour and cornmeal. Whisk in the sugar, baking powder, and salt. In another bowl, whisk together the milk, sour cream, and eggs. Stir the wet ingredients into the dry ingredients just until mixed. Stir in the butter. Pour the batter into an 8-inch (20-cm) square baking pan and bake until a toothpick inserted in center comes out clean, 30–35 minutes. Cut into squares.

**MAKES 8 SERVINGS**

## Enchilada Sauce

**New Mexican chile powder,** 2 tablespoons

**Ground cumin,** 2 teaspoons

**Dried oregano,** ½ teaspoon

**Ground cinnamon,** ½ teaspoon

**Olive oil,** 2 tablespoons

**Yellow onion,** ½ cup (2½ oz/70 g) finely chopped

**Garlic,** 1 tablespoon minced

**All-purpose flour,** 2 tablespoons

**Tomato sauce,** 1 can (15 oz/425 g)

**Vegetable broth,** 2 cups (16 fl oz/500 ml)

**Brown sugar,** 1 tablespoon

**Sea salt and freshly ground pepper**

In a small bowl, combine the chile powder, cumin, oregano, and cinnamon, and set aside. In a saucepan, warm the oil over medium heat. Add the onion and sauté until it begins to brown, 4 minutes. Add the garlic and sauté for 10 seconds. Stir in the flour and spice mixture and cook, stirring constantly, 1 minute. Whisk in the tomato sauce, broth, and brown sugar and bring to a simmer. Reduce the heat to low, cover, and cook, stirring frequently, until the sauce is thickened and bubbly, 10 minutes. Season to taste with salt and pepper.

**MAKES 3 CUPS (24 OZ/750 G)**

## Kale Pesto

**Lacinato kale,** 2 cups packed (2 oz/60 g), chopped

**Parmesan cheese,** 2 tablespoons grated

**Garlic,** 2 teaspoons finely chopped

**Lemon juice,** 2 teaspoons

**Olive oil,** ¼ cup (2 fl oz/60 ml)

**Sea salt and freshly ground pepper**

Bring a small saucepan of water to a boil. Add the kale and cook until tender, 2 minutes. Drain in a colander, rinse with cold water, and press the greens to remove as much water as possible. Place the kale, cheese, garlic, and lemon juice in a mini food processor or blender. With the machine running, slowly add the oil and blend until smooth. Season with salt and pepper.

**MAKES ABOUT ⅔ CUP (4 OZ/125 G)**

## Mango-Avocado Salsa

**Ripe mango and ripe avocado,** 1 *each*, diced

**Green onion,** 1, thinly sliced

**Jalapeño chile,** ½—1, finely minced

**Rice vinegar,** 2 tablespoons

**Extra-virgin olive oil,** 1 tablespoon

**Hot sauce,** ½ tablespoon

**Sea salt and freshly ground pepper**

In a bowl, gently mix together all of the ingredients. Season to taste with salt and pepper.

**MAKES ABOUT 2¼ CUPS (6¼ OZ/190 G)**

## Poached Eggs

**Large eggs,** 4

**White wine vinegar,** 4 teaspoons

**Sea salt,** 1 teaspoon

Crack the eggs into small ramekins or tea cups. Fill an 8-inch (20 cm) frying pan with water. Bring the water to a boil, add the vinegar and salt, and stir to dissolve. Turn off the heat. Quickly and gently, slide each egg into the water. Cover the frying pan, move it off the burner, and set a timer for 3½ minutes.

**MAKES 4 EGGS**

# Index

# weldon**owen**

1045 Sansome Street, Suite 100, San Francisco, CA 94111
www.weldonowen.com

Weldon Owen is a division of
## BONNIER

**WELDON OWEN, INC.**

President  Roger Shaw
Senior VP, Sales and Marketing  Amy Kaneko
Director of Finance  Philip Paulick

Associate Publisher  Jennifer Newens
Associate Editor  Emma Rudolph

Creative Director  Kelly Booth
Art Director  Marisa Kwek
Senior Production Designer  Rachel Lopez Metzger

Production Director  Chris Hemesath
Associate Production Director  Michelle Duggan

Photographer  Kimberley Hasselbrink
Food Stylist  Lillian Kang

**WEEKNIGHT VEGETARIAN**

Conceived and produced by Weldon Owen, Inc.
In collaboration with Williams-Sonoma, Inc.
3250 Van Ness Avenue, San Francisco, CA 94109

**A WELDON OWEN PRODUCTION**

Copyright © 2015 Weldon Owen, Inc. and Williams-Sonoma, Inc.

All rights reserved, including the right of reproduction
in whole or in part in any form.

Printed and bound by RR Donnelley in China

First printed in 2014

10 9 8 7 6 5 4 3 2 1

Library of Congress Cataloging in Publication data is available

Hardcover Edition ISBN 13: 978-1-61628-811-2
Hardcover Edition ISBN 10: 1-61628-811-6

Paperback Edition ISBN 13: 978-1-61628-815-0
Paperback Edition ISBN 10: 1-61628-815-9

## ACKNOWLEDGMENTS

Weldon Owen wishes to thank the following people for
their generous support in producing this book:
Amanda Anselmino, Morgan Bellinger, Casey Catelli,
Emily Garland, Taylor Louie, Eve Lynch, Nico Oved,
Elizabeth Parson, Abby Stolfo and Alexa Weibel

## PHOTO CREDITS

All photos by Kimberley Hasselbrink except pages 61, 71, 76,
96, 108, 116, 120, 126, 153, and 165 by Katie Newburn